T0114009

ABUNDANCE UNLEASHED

ALSO BY CHRISTIAN MICKELSEN

Change The World:
And Make Big Money Teaching,
Training, and Serving Humanity

Get Clients Today:
How to Get a Surge of New, High Paying
Coaching Clients Today & Every Day

How to Quickly Get Started as a Personal Coach:
Get Paid Big Money to Change People's Lives

ABUNDANCE UNLEASHED

OPEN YOURSELF TO MORE MONEY, LOVE, HEALTH, AND HAPPINESS NOW

Christian Mickelsen

HAY HOUSE, INC.
Carlsbad, California • New York City
London • Sydney • New Delhi

Copyright © 2017 by Christian Mickelsen
Instant Miracle™ and Instant Miracle Technique™ are trademarks of
Christian Mickelsen and Future Force Inc. All rights reserved.

Published in the United States by: Hay House, Inc.: www.hayhouse.com®
Published in Australia by: Hay House Australia Pty. Ltd.: www.hayhouse.com.au
Published in the United Kingdom by: Hay House UK, Ltd.: www.hayhouse.co.uk
Published in India by: Hay House Publishers India: www.hayhouse.co.in

Cover design: Bradford Foltz
Interior design: Nick C. Welch
Interior photos/illustrations: Nick C. Welch

**Cataloging-in-Publication Data on file
with the Library of Congress**

Tradepaper ISBN: 978-1-4019-5346-1
1st edition, August 2017

Printed in the United States of America

*This book is dedicated to anyone who's ever
felt scared, alone, small, unlovable, vulnerable,
or unlikely to ever amount to much. You are
stronger than you know. You're capable of more
than you could ever imagine. Your true power has
been hidden by the challenges of your childhood.
But it's ready to be revealed in its full glory as
we unlock your true potential and get you on
the fast track to your ultimate destiny.*

CONTENTS

INTRODUCTION

Money, Love, Sex, Health, Happiness, Fame, and Fortune

Money, love, sex, great health, fame, fortune, success, and happiness can all be yours. The only proof you need is the fact that others have them. And contrary to popular belief, other people don't really have an advantage over you. Yes, they might be born with better looks, parents, and connections, and more wealth, but these "advantages" aren't the keys to success.

I grew up on welfare in a nothing neighborhood, and over several years of hard work, turned myself into a multimillionaire. It wasn't easy. I had ups and downs. I worked my way through college only to have doors closed on me as soon as I graduated. I got caught up with the wrong crowd and was arrested more than once. Then I turned things around and found a better way. Over the years, I've achieved a life beyond my wildest dreams. Now I'm a sought-after business expert and a powerful spiritual healer.

My desire to help people find peace started when I was growing up. My parents fought a lot. They got really angry and intense. They screamed, argued, pushed, shoved. They broke things. And as a little kid, I was really scared. I kept thinking, *What's happening? And why? How can I make them happy again? How can I help them? How can I make them love each other? How can I make them be loving to each other? What can I do?* I felt powerless and would run crying into my older brother's room, where it felt safe, to get away from the noise. Seeing my parents fighting put me on a quest for peace: *How can I help people? How can I take the pain away?*

I got into the pattern of helping because my mother used to come to me for comfort and advice. At age 6, 7, 8, 9, 10—my entire life. Seeing her in pain killed me. I wanted to help her all the time. And that desire spread to others. I wanted to help people get along. *Why can't people get along?* I wondered. *Why are people fighting? Why is there war in the world?* And I realized my quest for peace, my desire to take other people's pain away, was really my own quest to take my own pain away. My desire for peace in the world was really a desire to find peace within myself.

Those things made me aware of the need to work on myself. I started studying personal growth in earnest when I was 12 years old and read *The Great Gatsby* for school. Jay Gatsby had written a list of things to work on to improve himself. *Wow,* I thought, *that's really cool.* And I made a list of things I wanted to improve about myself. From that day forward, I was hooked, driven toward working on my personal growth. I read every book I could find on the subject, and I haven't stopped since.

My lifelong search for personal growth has led me to visit the pyramids at Teotihuacan with Don Miguel Ruiz and get certified in neurolinguistic programming (NLP) and hypnotherapy. I learned to do The Work of Byron Katie, and even got to work with her personally at one of her events. I've been blessed to ask questions of Abraham onstage with Esther Hicks. I've studied closely with many leaders in personal growth—including Tony Robbins, Wayne Dyer, Deepak Chopra, Eckhart Tolle, David Hawkins, and Dan Millman—some of whom have become friends over the years. I've learned dozens of healing modalities, become a Reiki Master Teacher, received many *diksha* blessings, gone on spiritual journeys with a shaman, and performed all sorts of studies on the inner self so that I could feel more peaceful, accepted, happy, and, ultimately, loved.

These books, studies, and trips to holy sites have been extremely helpful and valuable, but nothing has helped me more than what I'll be sharing in this book—healing and abundance techniques I've developed, been gifted with, and brought to hundreds of thousands of people all around the world. Every page of this book is infused with powerful healing energy to uplift your mind, body, and soul. Just by reading, you're going to become richer, happier, and healthier, and fall more in love with your-self, the world, and everyone in it. That is my hope for you, and the reason I wrote this book.

The first six chapters are best read sequentially, because they'll set you up for the rest of the book. You'll take four Abundance Assessments™—love, wealth, health, and time—to determine areas where you might want to work on, and you can focus on them throughout the book. I'll introduce you to the Peace Process, a technique you can practice on your own to release fears and limiting beliefs that block you from having all you want in your life, often in a matter of minutes (sometimes even seconds). I'll explain Instant Miracle™, a healing technique I often use in conjunction with the Peace Process. This technique was gifted to me by my spirit guides and can heal fears, limiting beliefs, and even health challenges instantly. You'll learn my 5-Step Rapid Success System to help you achieve your goals and manifest more abundance. You'll also find links to my website so you can watch and heal along with others and get access to bonus videos.

The remaining six chapters can be read sequentially, or you can select one that appeals most to you in that moment. If, for instance, you have areas you'd like to work on based on your Love Abundance Quiz, you could first read Chapter 9: You Are Loved, Deeply Loved. Or maybe you want to work on time abundance, in which case, you could focus first on Chapter 10: We Have All the Time in the World. Of course, you'll want to read all the chapters in this book to take full advantage of its teachings. And after finishing, you can pick up this book again and again to help you set new goals and unearth and release emotional and physical blocks that are getting in your way.

Abundance is everywhere! With a little creativity and determination, there's no limit to what's possible. This book is the shortcut to having what you want. If you're ready for an amazingly rich and rewarding life, be sure to read every page as if your life depends on it, because the *quality* of your life certainly does.

CHAPTER 1

THANK GOD, WE'RE RICH!

I saw my dad cry only once in my life. It was the day he was forced to leave the house when my parents divorced. As a nine-year-old, I thought "divorce" was the way to stop all the fighting. I thought it was supposed to be a good thing, until my dad started crying. After he was gone, the fighting stopped for a little while, until my mom's new boyfriend moved in. They fought even more than my parents had.

Since my mom was now raising four kids on a waitress's income, she set us up on welfare programs—free lunches at school, food stamps, and food from a local food pantry. Until that point, my only experience with money was that it caused endless fighting, some of which ended in slammed doors and dishes flung across the room. But after my parents' divorce, our money problems were even worse.

We didn't have enough money to pay the utilities. Some months it was like musical chairs, wondering what would be turned off next—the gas or the electricity, the water or the garbage pickup. If the garbage wasn't paid, then it would be left out on the curb, piling up embarrassingly for weeks. Sometimes, when the water was shut off, we'd have to skip baths. That was the worst, because then I had to go to school stinky with messy hair and dirty clothes. Other times, when the gas was shut off in the dead of winter in Chicago, we'd huddle by the electric space heater for warmth. One time, my brother's bed caught on fire because he had the heater too close to his bed. Often the cold made for a terrible night's sleep, leaving me groggy and tired at school.

The lack of money began to affect my sense of self-worth. At school, when the lunch bell rang, most kids were laughing and excited to eat. Not me. I had to stand in line to get a free lunch for the poor. Usually, it would be something like a baloney sandwich with mustard. I didn't like mustard. But the food wasn't the worst part. It was standing in line to get the lunch, because everyone could see who the "poor kids" were. It felt like my secret shame was on full display in front of my whole school.

I was 10 years old the first time I stood in the free lunch line. I noticed that everyone stood there with their heads down—their hair messy, shoulders slumped— feeling lower than the "regular" kids, lower than dirt. I looked around the cafeteria and made eye contact with a kid from my class. He started to smile, until he realized which line I was in, and then he looked away. He probably just didn't know how to act around people in the "poor kids" line, but I took his reaction to mean he thought I wasn't good enough to be his friend. I assumed all the other kids felt the same way, and from then on I became super shy, afraid to talk to anybody at school because I thought nobody wanted to be my friend. And that became the reality I manifested for myself.

I felt ashamed of being poor. Kids teased me about my ragged, old, long-out-of-style, secondhand (and third-hand) clothes, first worn by my two older brothers. It seemed all the poor kids had ugly clothes, and these kids didn't tend to be the most popular. I desperately wanted to be liked and accepted, but this didn't seem like the fast track. Eventually, I started skipping lunch and would find a place to hide at school where no one would find me until lunch was over.

I thought being rich would solve my problems. This kid in my class, Ron, got brand-new fruity-smelling markers. Everyone wanted to be his friend and borrow his markers. I wished I were rich so I could get markers too, and then everyone would want to be my friend. I assumed Ron's life was easy. However, looking back, who knows? I'm sure he had his own stuff to work through. We all do. Maybe he never knew who his real friends were because the friends he had liked him only for what he had or what he could give them. We think people with more money have it easier, and in a lot of ways they might, but in the end, we're all human. We all have insecurities, worries, fears, doubts, and challenges in life. And it's time to let them go. And if you want more money, I'll show you how to get it.

WE MANIFEST OUR DESIRES . . . AND OUR FEARS

Our interpretation of any given event shapes our reality, and if we attach the wrong meaning to that event, it can mess us up. As a kid, I associated wealth with popularity and saw it as the solution to life's problems. In my early adult life, I worried about money all the time. I thought I'd stop worrying once I made a certain amount of money or had "enough" in the bank, but once I was making good money, I still worried. That's when I realized my worrying had nothing to do with my external circumstances.

I didn't know it back then, but I was terrified of feeling the shame I'd experienced as a kid. I was running from that feeling by trying to get rich and making sure people didn't think I was poor. Underneath all of my money worries was actually a fear of feeling shame. Even though my money fears drove me to pursue wealth, paradoxically, it wasn't until I let go of my fear of shame that massive amounts of money flooded into my life and my bank account.

I believe we can manifest what we desire if we focus on that desire, believe we can have it, and are hungry for it, without being needy for it. Neediness pushes away the health, wealth, and love we want to bring into our lives. I also believe we manifest our greatest fears if we worry about them obsessively. Worrying is like praying for what we don't want. We manifest into our lives the things we most desire and the things we most fear—or a watered-down version of the two. For example, if we're worried about money and being homeless, and we also dream about being rich and winning the lottery, those two energies collide, and we end up with a diluted version of each. The reality isn't as bad as we feared and not as great as we dreamed.

Now, in my forties, with more money than I ever dreamed of, I can see that the fights about money my parents had weren't really about money. The money challenges pushed buttons they had about not feeling secure, trusted, heard, valued, important, and loved. All of these underlying hot buttons we have can be healed. But without any tools to work together to let go of those insecurities (tools I'll be sharing with you in this book), my parents were doomed to struggle in their relationships, as many people do.

GRATITUDE PRACTICE

A key element to attracting what you want into your life is gratitude. A few years ago, I spent a lot of time focusing on gratitude. At the same time, my income increased by more than a million dollars in one year. Incredible! But as amazing as it was to have so much money, my gratitude made a much bigger difference to the quality of my life. The richest person on Earth isn't the person with the most money, it's the person with the most gratitude.

The richest person on Earth isn't the person with the most money, it's the person with the most gratitude.

As I look back, even when I was on welfare I was rich, or at least I could have been had I been grateful for what I had. Instead, I resented having to fend for myself, cooking dinner for myself every night by the time I was 12 years old. We got most of our food from the local food pantry—a lot of mac and cheese, one of the only things I could make, so I ate a lot of it. I grew to hate mac and cheese. Now I have three little girls and a private chef, and guess what my daughters want for lunch and dinner almost every day? That's right, mac and cheese!

I really believe that, for most of modern civilization, there's no such thing as "poor." If you have enough food, water, shelter, air, and sunlight to keep your body alive, then you're rich. Every single day of your life, God has provided enough for you to be alive. So both my wife and I say, "Thank God, we're rich!" Many of my clients' mind-sets have shifted significantly by practicing gratitude this way. Recently, one of my clients, Michelle, went from making $20,000 a year for 10 years to getting clients that each pay her $20,000 per year. She's crushing it. She was grateful at $20,000 a year. And she's even more grateful now.

Maybe you're thinking, *That's good for you, or your clients, but how can I go around saying, "Thank God, I'm rich," if I'm not rich? If I don't feel it, I can't own that because it feels wrong. It makes me uncomfortable."* If you can't see yourself as being rich even now, it's going to be hard to manifest more money into your life. If you see yourself as poor or even middle-class, then you're going to push away or dismiss anything that conflicts with that identity. Even if more money is coming in, you'll say, "Oh, yeah, that's good, but that's just going to go to paying off bills. I'm not rich." I'm not talking about denying your money challenges or your money reality. Hear me out, because one of the most important things you can do to manifest abundance in your life is to start seeing yourself as rich.

I'm not talking about "pretending to be rich," while deep down thinking you're not. I'm talking about really seeing and believing that it's true right now. I'm also not talking about seeing how you're rich in friendships and in spirit (though it's great to be abundant in those areas too).

Think about how much God has already provided for us. The sun warms our planet just enough to keep us alive but not so much that we're all toast. That is a miracle in and of itself, and something to be extremely grateful for. We have all the air we've ever needed, all the water we've ever needed. And even if some days we didn't have any food, we've always had enough to stay alive. I was rich when I was on welfare, wearing worn-out old clothes and eating mac and cheese, even though I didn't have brand-new fruity-smelling markers. We're all rich, but we're mostly blind to it. And anything we have beyond air, food, water, and shelter is a massive bonus.

Here's how to own the feeling of being rich even more. Any time you're paying a bill, say, "Thank God, I'm rich." Instead of being upset about having to pay for things, be grateful that you *can* pay and that you *chose* to pay. Be grateful that you *have* electricity instead of being upset that the rates have gone up. Be grateful for your car and all the places it can take you instead of feeling frustrated about having to make your car payment.

Even when an unexpected expense comes up, say, "Thank God, I'm rich." Even if you don't know how you're going to pay for it, say "Thank God, I'm rich," and allow your higher power to help bring the money into your life.

Seeing yourself as rich is a much more powerful identity than seeing yourself as "middle-class" or "poor." As you retrain your mind, you open to greater appreciation and resourcefulness. This is part of an overall mind-set shift to massive appreciation. The richest person on Earth isn't the one with the most money, it's the one with the greatest appreciation.

LOOK FOR WHAT'S AMAZING

I have a friend who, whenever we go to a restaurant, is always finding fault with her food. "Oh, they overcooked this." Or "I asked for this, and got that." Or "This waiter is so slow. He should have brought me a second drink before I finished my first one."

You can always find what's not right. If you're looking for it, you can find it. Easily. You can also look for what's amazing. If you train your eyes to see what's remarkable, what's special, what's a miracle, then you will find miracles. The sun rising every day and warming the Earth is a miracle. Earth is the only planet in our solar system that has mild-enough weather for humans to survive. Our very existence is a miracle. Seeds that lay dormant for years can be eaten or, years later, planted and watered and then turn into trees and flowers, some of which grow fruits and vegetables that we can eat. Together as a society we've created shared resources that are available to most of us for minimal costs or free, such as libraries, roads, electricity, the Internet, running water, and indoor plumbing. Things you might be taking for granted are things that even the richest people alive didn't have access to just a couple of generations ago. We are swimming in oceans of abundance. There are so many miracles in this world, so much beauty, so much amazingness.

THE PRAYER OF ABUNDANCE

In my life, and in my coaching practice, I've found that saying a prayer of abundance helps me realize the beauty and miracles in my life, and increases my gratitude for what I have. Please note that I'm talking about saying a prayer "of" abundance and not a prayer "for" abundance. You already have massive abundance in your life, and much more is on the way.

Most people pray asking for things. "Please help me find a job." "Please heal my sick mom, aunt, cousin." There's nothing wrong with these types of prayers. But the prayers I find that work best are prayers of gratitude, because those prayers aren't coming from a needy energy. "Thank-you prayers" are awesome because they help you to get in touch with what's already great in your life. Gratitude is a great space to be in. It feels amazing and it's magnetically attractive to more of the good things we want. Next time you pray, instead of an "asking-for" prayer, try saying a prayer of gratitude or thanks. "Thank you, God, for all of the blessings and abundance in my life. Amen."

And if you want to take it to the next level, start adding in prayers of gratitude *in advance* for all the things you're looking forward to having in your life.

Here's an example: "Thank you, God, for all the wonderful people in my life, for all the love in our hearts, for all of the smiles on our faces. Thank you for all the blessings and abundance in our lives. Thank you for all the oceans and avalanches of abundance tumbling into our lives in ever-increasing amounts day after day. Amen."

You can also be more specific: "Thank you, God, for the inspiration to write this book with joy and ease. Thank you for helping make this book a big hit that touches the lives of every man, woman, and child on Earth now and for as long as these ideas and strategies are useful for humanity. Amen." Think of some things you want to bring into your life and practice praying in appreciation for them in advance.

CHAPTER 2

TEST YOUR ABUNDANCE LEVELS

In my experience, people who aren't getting what they want or aren't as happy, free, openhearted, healthy, or wealthy as they want to be, usually have blocks to their abundance. After seeing these blocks time and time again with my clients, I created four Abundance Assessments to help them realize and appreciate the miracles they already had in their lives and manifest even more abundance. I've included these Assessments in this chapter so you can see how abundant you are in your life right now, pinpoint the areas where you might be blocked, and open the floodgates to experience more of what you want right now. Then, as you go through the rest of the book, you can retake these tests to see how much progress you're making.

There are four Abundance Assessments—one each for wealth, love, health, and time. For each question, select an answer on the continuum from low abundance (1) to high abundance (10). There's no "right" answer other than what feels right for you. You don't need to impress anyone with high numbers. You don't need to overanalyze. Look for what's true for you, go with your gut, and move on to the next question.

TEST YOUR ABUNDANCE

For this exercise, you'll need a piece of paper and something to write with to keep track of your points. If you want to take the Abundance Assessments online, so you can save your scores and note your progress over time, go to www.AbundanceScore.com. Bonus: if you take the Assessments online, you'll also get exclusive access to a special Infinite Abundance training video.

Wealth Abundance Assessment™

Score each item from 0 to 10, add your scores, and then divide the total by 10.

0	1	2	3	4	5	6	7	8	9	10

I don't have enough money; I never have enough money.	I have all the money in the world; I am swimming in oceans of abundance.
When I see things I really want, I immediately try to make myself satisfied with what I already have or tell myself it's wrong to want so much.	When I see things I really want, I give them to myself; or if it's beyond my current means, I consistently focus on manifesting it.
Even when I get money, I'm not a good steward of money. I don't invest it wisely, and I don't build up my savings.	I'm a good steward of money. I save and invest wisely as I'm guided to do.
I have a hard time spending money on myself and/or loved ones.	I love spending money on myself, my loved ones, and even strangers.
I resent paying my bills, my taxes, and any obligations that don't bring me immediate joy.	I gratefully pay my bills, my taxes, and all my obligations and take joy in knowing they contribute to a wondrous lifestyle that few truly appreciate.
I rarely contribute time and money to charitable causes, and I feel guilty about it.	I donate the perfect amount of time and money to charitable causes.
I don't feel secure financially, and I always worry I won't have enough money.	I feel completely financially secure, and I know I'll always be well taken care of in the future.
I work to make sure things are fair for myself and others and that I get what I'm due.	I let go of fairness and look for how I can contribute and create more value for others and the world.
I worry about money all of the time. No matter how much I do or don't have, it never feels like enough.	I live in a constant state of gratitude.
I see myself as poor or middle class.	I thank God I'm rich!

Health Abundance Assessment™

Score each item from 0 to 10, add your scores, and then divide the total by 8.

0	1	2	3	4	5	6	7	8	9	10

I feel very unhealthy.		I feel extremely healthy, vibrant, and alive.
I get sick or injured frequently.		I am extremely healthy the vast majority of the time.
If people around me get sick, it's extremely likely that I'll get sick too.		I stay healthy no matter what's going around and no matter who I know has it.
If I get sick or injured, it seems to take me a long time to recover.		If I do ever get sick or injured, I bounce back and recover extremely quickly.
I am not very physically active and avoid being active whenever I can.		I am highly physically active on a regular basis, and I enjoy it.
My body is stiff with lots of aches and pains.		My body moves with grace and ease.
I eat a lot of unhealthy foods.		I eat loads of healthy foods.
I feel guilty about my meal choices, snacks, and desserts that I eat.		I feel great about my meal choices, snacks, and desserts that I eat.

Love Abundance Assessment™

Score each item from 0 to 10, add your scores, and then divide the total by 9.

0	1	2	3	4	5	6	7	8	9	10

I hold back who I am and what I will say with most people.	I am fully self-expressed and truthfully, authentically myself with everyone in my life.
I feel shy and reserved around most new people.	I am open and friendly toward everyone I meet.
If someone hurts my feelings, they must have done something wrong, and they need to apologize for it.	No one can hurt my feelings but me, and when that happens, I work on healing myself.
If my emotional needs aren't being met by someone, I get frustrated, blame them, and act out.	I take responsibility for my emotional needs and make sure they are met, sometimes through a variety of relationships.
I'm afraid the people I love most are going to leave me.	I never even think about people leaving me. Why would anyone do that? And if someone did, I trust in the universe that it's the best for everyone.
I love to give and contribute to people I care about, and I expect others to equally give and contribute back to me; it's only fair.	I love to give and contribute to people I care about with zero expectation of anything in return.
I have old resentments with my friends and family.	My relationships are fresh and new no matter how long we've known each other.
Why would anyone love me?	I am extremely lovable.
My heart is closed to everyone with few exceptions.	My heart is wide open to the world and everyone in it.

17

Time Abundance Assessment™

Score each item from 0 to 10, add your scores, and then divide the total by 7.

0	1	2	3	4	5	6	7	8	9	10

I worry about the future, getting things done, and getting to the next level.		I live in the present moment.
I don't enjoy the activities I do; I just do them to get them done.		I enjoy everything I do.
I'm never satisfied with how much I accomplish.		I'm very pleased with how much I accomplish.
I feel overwhelmed and stressed.		I feel peaceful and relaxed.
I'm always in a hurry to get to places.		I get where I need to be and feel good about it.
My mind is so cluttered with things I have to do that I don't even have time to think.		My mind is free and clear for new ideas and opportunities.
I feel there is never enough time in my life.		I feel an abundance of time.

As a general guideline, if you scored from 0 to 4 on a question in the quiz or on a quiz as a whole, my guess is that you have a lot of struggle in those areas, which might then be the first ones you'll want to work on using the tools in this book. If you scored from 5 to 7, your life is pretty solid in those areas, but there's still room for improvement. I recommend working through any blocks you may have so you can open yourself up to even more abundance. If you scored from 8 to 10, you can rest assured that in those areas you're in really great shape, your life is abundant, and you can serve as an amazing role model for other people.

Now that you've taken these Assessments, you have an idea of what you might want to work on that might be getting in the way of your manifesting what you want. I'll be sharing powerful tools with you in this book, including Instant Miracle, the Peace Process, and the 5-Step Rapid Success System, all of which will help you speed up the process of getting everything you want. Certain chapters in the book are devoted to an area of abundance. Chapter 1 focuses on wealth abundance. Chapter 9 focuses on love abundance, and Chapter 10 on time abundance. And throughout the book, I offer client stories and my own stories of health abundance.

When you've finished the book, I recommend taking the Assessments again to see how much progress you've already made. As you incorporate these tools into your life, you can retake these Assessments to help you take stock, set new goals, and create more miracles.

YOU ALREADY HAVE WHAT YOU WANT

It may not feel like it, but whatever you want, you already have. And by letting go of the feeling that you lack something, you can start to find that you already have it, or at least some of it. Let's look at health abundance.

If you want to be healthy, start appreciating how healthy you already are. Start appreciating what's already working in your body. The human body needs to be 99 percent healthy just to be alive. So if you're alive—and I assume you are if you're reading this—then your body is so, so, so, soooo healthy. Think about what it takes to be alive. All the organs, cells, our nervous system, chemical reactions, atoms, and molecules that need to be working in harmony just to keep us taking our next breath.

And while, for many of us, there are things that aren't working 100 percent optimally yet—some back pain, digestive issues, fatigue, or whatever the case may be—the fact that you're alive means that so much is working right.

Now if you're in pain, or something isn't working optimally, it's easy to focus on what's "wrong." Pain can scream out for attention. I don't want you to deny that something could be working better than it is right now. We don't want to pretend a problem doesn't exist, or ignore it. And obviously seek medical attention when needed. To speed up healing, what we want to do is focus on what's already working great, and be really appreciative of that. And be grateful in advance that more good health is coming our way. So, for example, if your left shoulder's hurting, instead of putting out negativity—"My shoulder hurts. My shoulder hurts"—try being thankful for what does work, that you have strong legs, or even that you can walk. When you practice gratitude for what's working great, your health abundance can increase substantially.

In the case of a sore shoulder, practicing gratitude may speed up your manifestation of good health. Even so, your shoulder may not heal as quickly as you'd like. There could be a purely physical reason for the shoulder pain, and with the right treatments it could be resolved. Or you could have something emotional you need to work through first. The body is a self-healing organism. It naturally wants to heal itself. If you get a cut, your body will heal it. If you come down with a cold, your body will get rid of it. But if something isn't healing, there could be a constriction of the flow of healing energy to that part of your body. That constriction is usually some sort of emotional pain that's somehow caught up in the injury.

One of my clients was in a car accident 19 years before working with me. She thought all her body pain was a result of the accident, and that she'd have to live with it for the rest of her life. When we tuned in deeper, we discovered she had lots of emotions tied up in that accident. She felt guilty for having ruined her parents' car. She felt ashamed of having made a big mistake in her driving. She was angry the accident happened to her and "ruined her life." After working on all these emotions with the Peace Process and Instant Miracle (which I'll discuss in Chapters 4 and 5) for 20 minutes combined, 80 percent of her aches and pains vanished immediately, and she felt better than she had in 19 years.

Regarding the sore shoulder, it's also possible that it isn't going to heal at all (or at least not for now), in which case it's better to make peace with the way things are than to be angry with the situation. When we're in pain, we tend to get angry, but sending hate toward hurt doesn't help. Send love instead.

There are blessings in everything, even an injured shoulder. Maybe the injury puts you on a different career path or gets you into physical therapy, where you meet your one true love. We never know for sure why things happen, but if you let go and allow life to unfold in its own divine way, you'll be able to see the blessing in your pain. If you look hard enough, the blessings are always there. Look for the gifts. You may have heard it said that things don't happen *to* us, they happen *for* us. With this attitude, you can see the gifts and miracles in everything, and you'll be able to manifest and achieve more of what you want. In the next chapter, we'll look at a key component to getting the things you want—a strategic, action-based plan.

If you want greater financial abundance, instead of suffering through feelings of inadequacy or fear, take a moment to appreciate what you have. If you want money, and you discover one dollar in your wallet, you have what you want. Maybe not as much as you want, but you do have what you want. If you get into a state of appreciation, you'll start attracting more money—maybe you'll realize you have an account you forgot about, or you'll find a $20 bill in an old pair of jeans, or you'll get a raise or a big bonus at work, or you'll attract some new, amazing opportunity into your life.

Recently, one of my coaching clients wrote me to share her experience of attracting a great opportunity seemingly out of nowhere. She works three-and-a-half days a week as an intervention specialist for gifted kids from kindergarten through fifth grade. She's been in her current position for just a few months, but she started working with me because she wants her own business.

> Hi, Christian,
>
> Ready for this? Yesterday I wrote down my idea for an education coaching program. I named the program Accelerating Leaders Platinum Program. Then I added a tagline: Lifting Up School Leaders to Let Their Light Shine!
>
> I put my vision out there, and the universe heard. Today, at school, the superintendent asked to chat. It's pretty uncommon for him to chat with teachers, so I had no idea what to expect. He started by asking me questions: "What's your vision? What do you hope to accomplish over the next few years? What are your life goals?" I had just printed out my vision that morning, so I boldly shared my coaching idea for administrators, explaining how I want to make a bigger impact on a larger scale—I want to teach administrators "how to fish," so they can do amazing work within their schools. He asked if I'd

like to be working next year as a principal in one of the elementary schools. I told him that would limit my vision. I want to affect many schools. Then he asked if I'd consider an administrative position to coach the staff in our district!

He made the following amazing, affirming comments: "I'm impressed by what I've seen from you the past few months, and the principal, who I work with all the time, is blown away." He said he wanted to "steal" me from the ESC (the county organization that hired me) and offer me a position in the district in a much larger capacity. "What can I offer you to take me up on this?" he asked. "I believe in your vision, and I share it. I want to create an administrative position for you, and perhaps have you be the superintendent of curriculum in a few years." Then he said the school would pay for my schooling to get that license.

Wowza! Right? I told him I want to work part-time only (he said no problem). I want benefits (no problem). I want to develop my coaching program and have the flexibility to travel and work on that vision (no problem).

Wow!! I'm excited, elated, overjoyed, and sooo grateful! So let's keep putting our amazing intentions out there and sending this phenomenal message to the universe that we're ready to heal the world!

Her story blew me away. She just put it out there—more time, doing work she loved, benefits! And she got more than she dreamed of. She went in with an attitude of gratitude. And as you can see in her letter, she's grateful for the opportunity the universe presented.

It can be hard to really get into that feeling of gratitude if your financial fears are too strong. We think that it's our financial situation that causes us to feel the fears. However, the situation just pushes a button inside us. With the Peace Process and Instant Miracle, you can get to peace with *any* financial situation, no matter how severe. The same applies for situations involving health, time, and love.

Once you get to peace, it's very easy to get to gratitude.

CHAPTER 3

THE 5-STEP RAPID SUCCESS SYSTEM

To get what you want in life, you have to be clear about what that is. If you want to be in a relationship, but you aren't sure about what you want in a partner, you're probably going to end up in a relationship that doesn't work out. Or maybe you know what you want, but you don't have a plan to get it. Then again, you might be clear about what you want and have a plan, but you lack the necessary skills to reach your goal. For example, you might want a relationship, but you lack communication skills. Or you might know what you want and how to get it, and have the necessary skills, but you don't have the support you need—you're in a negative environment. Maybe your friends are telling you, "Men suck, relationships suck. We're all going to be single and alone for the rest of our lives, but at least we have each other." That doesn't help. And, finally, you might have all these elements down cold, but you need to master a few things in your own psychology to achieve your goal. Maybe you don't feel deserving, or you're fearful about going up and talking to somebody you don't know, or you're afraid to have your heart broken again.

Mastering the five areas of focus in the 5-Step Rapid Success System will change your life and help you achieve anything you want. I developed this five-part methodology 12 years ago in the early years of my life-coaching business. It's helped me to live an amazing life, and helped thousands of other people achieve their goals too. I want to share this system with you here.

The steps are:

1. Clarify your direction.
2. Strategize your actions.
3. Upgrade your skills.
4. Optimize your environment.
5. Master your psychology.

If you're not getting what you want, whatever it is—relationships, great health, money, career, success—read through the following five areas to see where you could be falling short.

Step 1: Clarify Your Direction

Despite any problems you're facing right now, or perhaps because of them, it's time to set goals. What do you want?

If you could wave a realistic magic wand, what would your life look like right now? In the next 3 months, 6 months, 12 . . . ? Most people don't really design their lives. They have a few hopes and dreams they don't take seriously enough to actually turn into goals.

It's time to get clear about what you want. What do you want to have (a new car, house, better communication in your marriage), do (learn to speak French, travel to Costa Rica, find love, lose weight, go on a spiritual retreat, change jobs), or become (an amateur basketball player, a humanitarian)?

Clarify Your Vision and Direction

I believe reaching your goals is inevitable if you're willing to keep taking the necessary actions to get there and work through the "inner" stuff that comes up along the way. When you become excited enough about your future and what's possible, you can make miracles happen. So let yourself just dream for a little while. Surrender to your dreams. Leave the "it's impossible" judgments to another time. Allow the part of yourself that plays *big* and is most connected to your authentic self to set the goal.

Now, take a few minutes to write down a few of your goals and dreams. Don't worry about *how* you'll make them happen. We'll get to that later.

Create a Vision Board

For this exercise, you'll need scissors, a glue stick, poster board, and pictures—from magazines, printed from the Internet, or that you have drawn yourself—that illustrate your goals and dreams. Make sure the pictures resonate with you, that you're happy, excited, or feel a sense of peace when you look at them. Your feelings play a huge part in manifesting your goals and dreams. Cut out the pictures, and paste them on the poster board. You might even get fancy and frame your vision board. Put it up somewhere that you'll naturally see it every single day.

Here's a fun story. Years before I met my wife, I made a vision board for the type of partner I'd like to have in my life. When I moved from Chicago to San Diego, I folded it up, tucked it away in a box of old pictures and letters, and eventually completely forgot about it. One day, my wife was decluttering and purging the contents of boxes that hadn't been opened in years, and there it was—my vision of my dream girl. She opened it up and, I won't lie, I felt a moment of panic. My wife has brown hair. What if I'd written that I wanted a blonde? But when I looked at it, I was surprised and amazed. It was my wife, every quality she possessed even down to her age, hair color, occupation, and interests. My wife was my dream girl, which I knew because I married her, but seeing that list reminded me of how magical the universe is.

Bottom line: when you know where you're headed, there's a sense of purpose that can be far greater and way more attention-grabbing than the problems of the past.

Step 2: Strategize Your Actions

Now that you know what you want, what do you think you might need to do to make it happen? I recommend taking the three most important goals you have and focusing on the top goal, or possibly all three, and making a plan to get there.

Ask yourself, "If I could break this goal down into three major chunks or milestones, what would they be?"

Here are a couple of examples of how you might break down one of your goals.

Goal: Climb Mount Kilimanjaro

Three major chunks:

1. Research. What will this goal entail in the form of time, money, and physical preparation? Note: Talk to people that did it and get their advice.

2. Get ready. Buy all the stuff I need. Book the travel. Do the physical preparation. Recruit buddies.

3. Execute. Travel, bring equipment, make the climb, bring friends.

I've never climbed a huge mountain and I don't really have any desire to, but if I were going to do it, that's how I'd break it down.

Let's try another example.

Goal: Be in a Relationship

Three major chunks:

1. Get clear about the kind of person I want to be with and the kind of relationship I'd like to have with that person.

2. Work on myself to release any fears, doubts, insecurities, and inadequacies that would keep me from feeling like I deserve the relationship I want, or prevent me from being able to naturally attract the kind of partner I'd like to be with.

3. Go to the places the type of person I'd like to attract would hang out. Show up with an open heart, with confidence, having fun, and unattached to "it" happening in a certain way, with a certain person, at a certain time—let the universe unfold naturally.

Now it's your turn. Ask yourself, "If I could break down my number-one goal into three major chunks or milestones, what would they be?" Then write down those milestones.

Step 3: Upgrade Your Skills

To achieve your goals, what skills would you need to learn or improve? If your goal is to climb Mount Kilimanjaro, those skills might be your sense of direction, your climbing skills, or your team and communication skills. If your goal is to find a job, you might need to improve your interviewing skills. If your goal is to find your soul mate, it might be your flirting skills.

Ask yourself, "To achieve the goal I want, what skill or skills could I improve to make achieving it even easier?"

Step 4: Optimize Your Environment

This is one of the most overlooked areas in life. The degree of challenge or ease involved in getting what you want in life is greatly influenced by your environment. Think about it. How hard is it to stick to your diet when everyone around you is eating chocolate chip cookies and ice cream? When I want to lose weight, I make sure there are *zero* dessert foods in my house. And I enlist my family's support. I've come to realize that I'm not stronger than chocolate. If it's near me, I'll eat it (especially dark chocolate—yum). If I'm going to eat high-caloric foods with little nutritional value while I'm on a diet, I want to do it consciously. I'll decide what I want, and then I'll have to leave the house to get it. Or the whole family will go out—we'll make dessert an event. As you can imagine, going out is a lot harder and a lot less tempting than having a plate of Oreos on the kitchen counter and passing by it every day.

It also helps that my five best friends are in pretty good shape. There's a saying in the personal-growth community that we become like the five people we spend the most time with. People in the community also say that if you take the average income of your five closest friends, it's most likely the same as yours. So if you want to make a change, one of the ways to optimize your environment is to start looking for friends who most resemble the way you want to be. That doesn't mean you have to get rid of your old friends, just that you might want to start adding new ones.

You can optimize your environment by adding to it or subtracting from it. You might optimize your mental environment by reading more good books. Books that inspire you, books that help you flesh out your vision of the goal you're trying to achieve. You can add inspirational audio programs and movies, and educational films. Or you might get rid of your TV (or at least cable TV) if you find yourself sitting around in "boredom" or "avoidance" by channel-surfing.

You can also optimize your physical environment by cleaning things up and tossing out all the old junk in your life, like old clothes and stuff you don't really ever use. You might be surprised that many items hold emotional memories, and we hold on to those things even if the memory was negative. Look at all the old clothes in your closet that you haven't worn for years. I'll bet some of those are from some special moment in time. But by letting go of those things, we can free ourselves up in ways unimaginable.

To optimize your social environment, you could ask your current friends to support you in your goals by cheering you on as you reach for them, and by being a good ear for you when things aren't going so well. Some people bump up against significant others, friends, or parents who are not supportive of their dreams. Sometimes the people in our lives are afraid we'll change and they could lose us. Just remember that however they respond to our big dreams, it isn't personal. It's about them, not you. I suggest using the Peace Process as an action step to help you be at peace with not needing their support or approval. Plus, any weird feeling that comes up within you because of how they respond can be released, and when you get to peace, the people around you often show up in a different way.

Years ago, I was working with a client named Marcy. She was starting a new business, and her husband was not very supportive. As much as she wanted her own business, she wanted to keep her husband happy even more. She felt hurt, angry, sad, and alone. I helped her make peace with her husband's upsets and rude comments. After 15 to 20 minutes of Peace Processing, she felt completely neutral to her husband's reactions, and she realized she could keep her business *and* her husband, because even though he was upset, she could find a way to be happy and help him be happy too.

On our next coaching call, she said, "I don't know what you did, but my husband is a whole new man! He hasn't said one negative thing about my business all week, and he completely cleared out the old trophies and other junk in the spare bedroom I use as an office. He said he wants me to have the space I need for my business without all his old stuff lying around. I was floored!"

When you change on the inside, the whole world changes on the outside. Even people who have treated you a certain way your whole life can magically transform before your eyes.

Before we go on to the final step, list five things you can do to optimize your environment (by addition or subtraction) that will help you achieve your goal. Which one will you do first? Once you decide, go do it. What better time than now?

Step 5: Master Your Psychology

Our mind and emotions—in the forms of doubt and fears—often present the biggest obstacles to our turning our problems into opportunities, and our opportunities into the exciting things we want in our lives. Our doubts and fears can keep us from taking action, from showing up in the world in a powerful and attractive way—one that's both confident and attracts what we want to us, getting us what we really want out of life.

So what do we do? One of my favorite tools for eliminating doubts and fears is the Peace Process. If you're experiencing blocks while doing these beginning five steps, or you find yourself making excuses, this system can help eliminate the feeling of being stuck, so that you can create the life of your dreams. The more at peace you become, and the more you surrender your fears, the higher the likelihood that you will have the life of your dreams. Creating the life of your dreams can be a scary and often lonely process. Stay the course. Do the work. Face your fear. On the other side is unimaginable freedom, happiness, and peace. I promise you.

CHAPTER 4

THE PEACE PROCESS

We attract situations into our lives that help us grow by gaining experience and getting stronger emotionally. We become stronger emotionally by facing our fears, feeling them fully, and moving on. If we don't resolve our emotional issues, we keep attracting repeat performances—similar relationships with the same kinds of partners, getting fired from multiple different jobs, having the same argument with our parents or partners, friends, or colleagues—over and over again.

Usually, when we're having a problem with a situation, there's something about the situation we don't like or are worried about. Most people respond by either trying to do something about it (a productive response) or trying to run away from it by distracting themselves (an unproductive response). My favorite distractions are chocolate and surfing the Internet. Other people might use beer, wine, sex, food, drugs, work, exercise, or TV.

I believe most of these addictions are caused not by the numbing agent of choice itself but by the painful emotions people aren't willing to face. Of course, the pleasure of the distraction feels good, but so does the escape, the relief from not having to feel the painful feelings pushed down deep inside. But these feelings are never fully buried. When we're running from our feelings, it's usually because we *are* feeling them to a certain extent. That's why we start running in the first place—why we start reaching for that piece of cake, the remote control, the beer, wine, or so on. Yet as hard as it can be to feel these emotions, it's so much easier if we understand they won't hurt or feel uncomfortable forever. The energy of emotions is like a storm. It runs its course and then it's gone. But only if we let ourselves feel those emotions fully.

EMOTIONS AREN'T LOGICAL

It's also easier to feel emotions when we realize there's no logic to them, that we don't need to get tangled in making sense of them. We just need to feel them, accept that they may make us feel a bit crazy, and know that the pain, discomfort, and craziness will pass. It's so much easier to understand how illogical emotions are, and that they'll actually blow over, if we look at how children handle them. Young kids are more open and honest. They haven't yet learned to hide their emotions. They simply react, feel the emotion, and let it go.

When my middle daughter, Zoey, was three, she spent 40 minutes crying and tantrumming because she wanted me to give her a ball. I gave her the ball just like she asked, and she started crying. I don't know why. For five minutes, I asked her repeatedly to tell me what was wrong and how I could fix it. For the next 20 minutes, I tried all sorts of things to console her. I even resorted to bribery—offering her chocolate, her favorite TV show, the game she most liked to play, a new toy—to see if it would work. Nothing would calm her down. Nothing except enough time to let it go.

Sometimes, very small things can cause huge upsets inside. If your partner doesn't offer you a glass of water when he gets one for himself, that might push a button that makes you feel unloved or uncared for. As a result, you feel angry, and underneath that anger, you feel hurt, because underneath *that*, you feel you're not good enough, and you don't want to face that feeling. Yet if you were to look that deep, and face that underlying feeling of pain and fear, it would release fully, completely, and permanently. And then the next time your partner got a glass of water for himself and not for you, you probably wouldn't even notice. Here's another big bonus: when you no longer have a "button" around something, you also stop attracting situations that will push your buttons. So the next time he gets himself a glass of water, he just might bring one for you too—without your having to say anything—just because you aren't energetically manifesting that old pattern.

But usually, most people don't tune in to their feelings at the deepest levels. Usually, it's just "You made me feel _____ " and "How could you be so selfish?" We blame others, project onto others, because feeling the truth is painful, and we're wired to avoid pain. This cycle of avoidance and blaming others repeats until we heal it, and release it.

LET GO OF ATTACHMENT

Let's look at how emotions might affect physical healing. If you have a health issue that you want to heal, it's common to layer on top of that issue all sorts of things that can make healing even harder. For example, we can add self-judgment because we feel we're "weak" or a "burden to others." We might feel angry with ourselves for poor past decisions that got us into this situation: "If only I had eaten better or exercised more."

The body naturally wants to heal itself. It's a self-healing machine. If you cut yourself, you bleed, scab over, and in a few weeks your skin is clear, as though nothing ever happened. Or if the cut is particularly bad, it heals but leaves a scar. If we break a bone, the bone heals and is usually even stronger than it was before the break. However, when we layer all sorts of emotional angst on top of the actual physical condition, we can lock things up and make it hard for the body to heal itself.

The more you can let go of the emotional anguish of having a health problem, the faster and easier your body can heal. If you let go of the shame, anger, blame, and so on, you increase your body's capacity for healing. Then there's "neediness." Sometimes, the hardest thing to let go of is the "neediness" around healing. This is the tricky one. If you can make peace with *not* healing, you're more likely *to* heal. Making peace with not healing doesn't mean you give up trying things that can help. It just means you're desiring to heal but not attached to it.

And the truth is that not everything is healable. Many things are, and they can heal much faster and easier than most people realize. The first step in that healing is to make peace with the emotional anguish about having a health condition and the emotional need for it to heal.

You can do both using the Peace Process.

THE PEACE PROCESS

When I'm helping people out of a really big problem, they're usually trying to figure out what to do. "What should I do, Christian?" they ask. "I could do this or that, or that or this. But if I do this, then that might happen. If I do that, then this might happen." Their thoughts are swirling, trying to figure things out. Unfortunately, the mind can't solve the real issue—fear.

All our fears are fears of feelings. Either physical feelings (like fear of getting burned or beat up) or emotional feelings (like shame or humiliation). Instead of trying to solve problems using logic, the first thing I help clients do is make peace with their biggest fears. Over the course of human history, overcoming fears used to seem impossible. We were told to just "get over it."

All our fears are fears of feelings.

Eventually, getting over it became possible, but only with years of therapy. Then new "mind technologies" came out in the late '70s, such as neurolinguistic programming (NLP) and hypnotherapy, that could sometimes help someone let go of behavioral and thought patterns in just a few hours. But now, with the Peace Process, you can release your fears often in a matter of minutes (sometimes even seconds), and you can do it on your own—no therapists or NLP practitioners that you need to pay.

With the Peace Process, we invite the feelings to be felt fully. We go into the eye of the hurricane where those feelings are most intense. We surrender and let the feeling we've zeroed in on completely take over and run its course. Approximately 99 percent of all issues that I Peace-Process for myself or others are resolved in a matter of minutes or hours. The remaining 1 percent have taken a lot of intense, long sessions, over several years, to finally work through. I've had only two fears I've had to work on that have been like that, which I'll talk about in Chapter 6.

The best time to work the Peace Process is right when you're feeling something come up. Sometimes that isn't practical. For example, right before you must go into a big meeting (or right during the meeting). In these cases, wait until you have 15 to 20 minutes to be by yourself, free of distractions, and then sit somewhere quiet and follow the steps below until you come to a place of peace. You'll be amazed at how quickly you can work through those feelings, and release the blocks that are getting in the way of your living your best life.

THE PEACE PROCESS: 7 STEPS TO PEACE IN ANY SITUATION

Let's work through the Peace Process right now. Find someplace quiet, make sure you're comfortable, and follow along with these seven steps.

Step 1: Find the Feeling. All feelings manifest in some part of your body. Think about the situation that's upsetting you, and notice where in your body the feeling is the strongest. Perhaps it will be in your throat, or your chest, or your stomach (these are the most common). But it could be in your hands, your head, or anywhere else in your body.

Step 2: Give It Attention. Instead of distracting yourself from the feeling, or trying to mentally solve the problem, just be present to the physical sensation of the feeling in your body.

Step 3: Be Unconditionally Loving (or Accepting). This feeling is here. It's a fact. It won't be here forever (though it might feel that way in the moment). For now, as long as it's here anyway, accept it. And if possible, send that feeling love.

Step 4: Focus on the Eye of the Storm. Inside the feeling in your body, there's an area of greatest intensity. Put your attention on that area and stay present to it, in an unconditionally loving or accepting way.

Step 5: Let It Breathe. As you give the feeling attention, it may shift in some way. It might become more intense, or less intense. It might move to different parts of your body. Stay with it and let it run its course. It's like an oil candle: the fuel needs oxygen to burn, but once the fuel's burned out, it's gone. Your attention is the oxygen and the feeling is the fuel. We never know how much fuel is in there. That's why we never know how long the Peace Process will take. Sometimes seconds. Sometimes minutes. And on very rare occasions, you might need several hours (or separate focused sessions, which I'll discuss in Chapter 6).

Step 6: Get to Peace. Stay with the feeling. Let it live, breathe, and grow. Let it move around if it needs to. Keep your attention on the most intense part in an unconditionally loving way. And eventually, you'll be at peace. Again, you'll usually arrive at peace in 5 to 10 minutes, sometimes faster, sometimes a bit longer.

Step 7: Enjoy Permanent Peace. After the feeling that's troubling you has run its course, you'll be left feeling neutral. That's peace. You might also be filled with joy or love. That's fun when that happens, but usually, you're left with a neutral feeling of peace.

To make sure you've cleared the negative feelings completely, think about the situation, problem, or fear that was bothering you. Notice whether you feel anything other than peace, love, or joy. If you do, repeat this process. Sometimes there are several layers that need to be processed. However, in most cases you're now free of the fear or angst that was causing unease and keeping you from being at your best. This is the place from which you want to make decisions or take action. This place of peace is where you can achieve your highest potential, where you feel permanent peace around a situation that may have totally owned you in the past.

The Peace Process is a very powerful and valuable way to transform your entire life into something quite magical, and to reclaim your greatest self. I've been using it for more than a decade now, and it's been a major blessing in my life, in my business, and in my relationships with my friends and family. I encourage you to give it a try. To watch examples of me taking people through the Peace Process, go to www .PeaceProcessNow.com. You'll also find a Peace Process guided meditation to download, so you can have me take you through the Peace Process.

In the next chapter, we'll look at the Instant Miracle Technique™, which can help speed up the Peace Process or, sometimes, resolve things instantly without even having to do the Peace Process at all.

CHAPTER 5

INSTANT MIRACLE

The Instant Miracle healing technique was gifted to me by my spirit guides more than a decade ago. It's changed my life and the lives of the people I work with from all over the world. The physical and emotional healings have been miraculous. And, oddly, it all started with shoplifting when I was 12.

I'd met a new friend, Tony, and on the way to school we stopped at a 7-Eleven so he could buy candy. I was waiting for him outside by the double glass doors when he came running out, a huge smile on his face.

"What's going on?" I asked. "Why are you so excited? What did you do? What's this all about?"

He tugged on my coat—"C'mon!"—and pulled me after him as he ran. When we were halfway down the street, he drew a giant grape Jolly Rancher candy from his sleeve. It took me a few seconds to realize . . . he stole it! I didn't know what to say or do about that. *Oh, my gosh!* I thought. *I would never do that. How could he? I mean, his father is a police officer!*

Over the next couple of months, we followed the same routine. We stopped at the store, and Tony shoplifted candy. A lot of candy. All that time, he kept daring me to shoplift too. At first, I refused. But I was on food stamps and didn't have any money to buy candy, and watching him eating candy every morning was killing me. So, finally, I took the dare. For a while, every morning on our way to school, we'd stop at the 7-Eleven and each steal a piece of candy. Then we got to the point where we were stealing three to five candy bars at a time. One night, I was lying in bed, and I felt this energy. I had a sense there were three presences in the room, and I heard a faint, nonjudgmental voice say, "If you steal again, you're going to get caught."

The next morning, Tony and I were on the way to the store, and I said, "You know what, I have a really bad feeling about this. Let's not take anything anymore."

He nodded. "I feel the same way. Let's stop. But let's do it one last time, and this time let's get something big."

I protested, but since we were both onboard with stopping, I figured one last time wouldn't hurt. Now, since we were kids, we weren't going after a *big* score in terms of cost. We were going for size, something larger than a candy bar. We went inside. Tony grabbed a giant bag of Fritos and stuffed it into his backpack, and I loaded a giant bottle of Gatorade in mine.

We were about to leave the store, almost at the door, when I spotted a roll of mixed-fruit Certs. I thought, *Let me grab that,* and slipped the roll up my sleeve. My friend made it out the door. I was right behind him when a hand grabbed the back of my jacket. The clerk had seen me steal the Certs and called the police.

I stood there, waiting for the police and wondering what they would do if they realized that not only had I taken the Certs, but I'd taken the Gatorade too. When the police came, I cried. They took me to my house, and since my mom was at work at the time, they left me with my brother, who's nearly 10 years older. They didn't tell my parents (and my brother didn't either), and the police never found my "big" score—the Gatorade.

THE GIFT OF INSTANT MIRACLE

That incident was the first time I connected with my spirit guides, and they were spot on. I really wished I'd listened to them. After that, I felt their presence a few times. Then, one night about 12 years ago, I found myself worrying about losing the money I had finally begun making steadily. Lying in bed, I felt the spirit guides' presence again, and I asked for help healing my new money worry. "Can you help me heal this?" They said yes, and almost immediately I felt this energy moving around and through me. When I tried to tune back into the fear, it was gone. All that was left was peace.

For years after that, I felt their presence. When I was in my twenties, I started asking for help with healing fears and blocks: "Hey, spirit guides, can you help me heal this thing?" I'd get a yes, and then I'd feel the energy flowing through me, and the healing would occur. After a while, I'd request healing, take a sudden huge healing breath, and the healing would occur. When I was in my early thirties, I felt a deep knowing that I could do the healing without my spirit guides' help. I asked them if such was true, and they said yes. Then I started using what I now call Instant Miracle on myself to heal fears, blocks, or even physical conditions. I'd feel the energy, take a huge healing breath, and that's it. It was gone.

I wondered if I could do this for my clients, so I tried it, and it worked great. I used it in person and over the phone. Then I thought, *Can I do this with a whole group of people at one of my live events?* I tried it out, and it worked again. After that, I began doing Instant Miracle more often. I felt blessed, humbled, and filled with joy at the changes Instant Miracle brought about. People said how different I seemed when presenting, and how powerful my events were. Now I do Instant Miracle at all my live events, for all the participants—even at my business-training events.

I have several live events where the main focus is healing using Instant Miracle, the Peace Process, and a few other amazing techniques. One of the events is called "Instant Miracle Experience." At this event, we release doubts and fears. We also heal physical issues—eliminating lifelong back pain, restoring hearing loss, improving eyesight, eliminating chronic migraines, and ending fibromyalgia. People fly in from all over the world to attend these events because the results are so incredible.

And no matter how many times I witness one of these Instant Miracles, I continue to be blown away.

At one of my seminars, a woman named Kathy came up on stage. She'd been suffering from chronic muscle and joint pain for as long as she could remember. She was 56 at the time and just wanted the pain in her body to "be quiet." Even though her body hurt, and on most days her pain was a level 10, she was still training to run in the Boston Marathon. Kathy got up every day and ran. She also had a very successful psychotherapy practice. By all accounts, she was successful, just in deep pain.

A lot of the work I discuss in this book is about just letting go and releasing all that old programming, both energetically and emotionally. When we release our fears, doubts, and limiting beliefs, we let go of the invisible chains holding us back and reclaim our power. Paradoxically, we must also surrender our need to have life show up in a specific way. I asked Kathy to surrender to *not healing*, because if she were attached to the healing happening, it was less likely that it would. The more you surrender to the area that's not healing, the more likely it is to heal. Sometimes things can heal instantly. Sometimes they can take time to heal. And sometimes it doesn't happen at all, and you have to surrender to that too.

I had a really strong feeling that when Kathy did Instant Miracle, things were going to open up and shift for her in ways she wouldn't expect. I really hoped the pain she felt physically could be completely resolved, because it sounded horrible, and the fact that she ran marathons anyway just showed the incredible amount of courage and strength she had inside her. Feeling our fear and doing it anyway is really, really tough. Feeling physical pain and doing it anyway is probably far tougher. That Kathy did so is a testament to her inner strength. It was time for her to appreciate her inner strength more so she could start seeing how powerful and amazing she really was.

At the time, I didn't know if Kathy's body was ever going to heal. It might have, or it might not have. The healing could have happened while we were together during those three days at the event. Or it might not have. The only mystery was time. At the event, we did Instant Miracle. She came to peace with her pain. And she surrendered to it. The next morning Kathy came bounding onstage. She was completely pain-free for the first time since she was six years old. I've been in touch with Kathy since that event, and I'm happy to report that her pain has never come back.

There are so many stories like Kathy's. Because of the huge success of Instant Miracle and the Peace Process, my team and I are in the beginning stages of performing third-party empirical studies so we can bring this amazing healing work to the world in an even bigger way. With a preponderance of evidence showing the effectiveness of these techniques, my goal is that Instant Miracle and the Peace Process be prescribed instead of addictive drugs that have side effects, or treatments that address only symptoms and not the root causes.

I also found I could bestow this gift upon others, which is when I developed Instant Miracle Mastery, a four-day live training and certification program I hold once a year. People from all over the world come to this training event to study how to heal themselves, their friends, their families, and— if they're coaches or healers—their clients. They learn the Peace Process, Instant Miracle, muscle testing, and ultrahigh-frequency-energy healing.

If you'd like to see Instant Miracle in action, go to www.InstantMiracleExperience.com to witness people healing many different issues. Not only will you see the healings occurring, but if you have similar challenges, the Instant Miracles will be working on you as you watch the videos.

DIVINE TIMING

It's important to understand that while these tools work really fast, and can change things very rapidly, not everything happens right away. We often take baby steps to mastery. Here's an example. When our daughter Nala was three, she watched an episode of *The Backyardigans*, a kids' show. The characters came upon a frozen lake, quickly invented ice skates, strapped them on, and instantly started skating beautifully, gliding all over the place. Nala got all excited and said she wanted to learn to skate. My wife, Chelsa, figured that since I was from Chicago I'd know how to skate and would be the perfect teacher. The thing is, I'd never gone ice-skating in my life. But Nala was so eager, I told them I'd give it a try.

When we got to the rink, I told Chelsa I wanted to skate around a few times before taking Nala. I skated around the rink twice—wobbly but getting the hang of it. After a couple of times around the rink, I stopped to get Nala, took her hand, and started out. Whoa! Immediately her feet slipped all over the place. She flailed around, then fell right on her butt. The look on her face was one of total shock that the first time she went ice-skating she didn't just like glide around the way they did on *The Backyardigans*.

Most people think they can achieve success much faster than it usually comes. You have to start as a beginner, then you become experienced. Then, eventually, you become advanced, then you become an expert, and, finally, you become a master. You can't go immediately to mastery. It would be great to go rock climbing for the first time and scale the wall with no problem. Or go ice-skating and sail around the rink. But it doesn't work that way. You've got to show up and do the work.

While Instant Miracle and the Peace Process can quickly heal your fears and free blocks to getting what you want, you'll often still need to put in the work to get there. If you're willing to do the work out in the world to get the things that you want, and you're willing to do the work on yourself, then whatever you want, whatever goals you might set for yourself, whatever you decide to create in your life will absolutely come to pass.

It just becomes a matter of time. How much time will it take to get to where you want to go? And how much action are you taking in the world, and how much are you working on yourself? All the while, it also depends on divine timing.

CHAPTER 6

MAKE FEARS DISAPPEAR FOREVER

Why do you think so many people are afraid of public speaking? Is it because they have to talk to people? That's probably not it, because we humans talk to each other all the time. People are afraid of public speaking because they're afraid they might mess up, look bad, and feel embarrassed, ashamed, or humiliated—or all the above. We aren't afraid of circumstances or activities. We're afraid of feelings.

It takes courage to feel those feelings. Even if you just feel the fear and don't do what you're afraid of, you're being courageous. Ideally, if I'm feeling fear or angst, I prefer to Instant-Miracle it and/or Peace-Process it, and then I can do whatever I was afraid of doing, but from a place of peace. The Instant Miracle and the Peace Process will help you face your feelings and heal your issues so you can let in more abundance, more flow, more prosperity. Of all the things I've Peace-Processed for myself and with clients, 99 percent have resolved in a matter of minutes or in some cases a few hours.

I usually do a much better job when I'm calm. Imagine giving a speech when you're terrified. How do you think you're going to perform? A little nervousness might help you make sure you're prepared—but with too much nervousness, no matter how prepared you are, you probably won't do your best. On the other hand, if you're relaxed, playful, focused, and in the moment, aren't you more likely to give a great speech? I believe we do our best work when we're "in the zone," "in the flow," and are present, peaceful, and alive.

But sometimes it doesn't work that way. Sometimes you need to feel the fear and do it anyway. "Feel the fear and do it anyway," as Susan Jeffers says, is great advice, but it's easier said than done. With smaller fears, taking action despite those fears isn't too difficult. Super-intense fears are a different story. In these cases, it takes extreme courage to feel the fear and do it anyway. After all, if you aren't afraid, you don't need courage.

I've had a few fears that took me years to resolve. During those years, I had to feel the fear and do it anyway. For example, I used to have a terrible fear of heights. On a scale of 1 to 10, my fear hovered at 100. When I first tackled my fear, I was 23. I hadn't developed the Peace Process or been gifted Instant Miracle, so I had to go with straight courage. I went to a seminar held by a famous success coach. He talked about going skydiving, and I thought, *Yes. Skydiving. That's what I need to do. I'll round up some people to go with me.* I walked up to other participants at random, asking, "You live around here? Let's all go skydiving." I gathered about 35 people to go with me. And after a bit of maneuvering, I found a schedule that worked for 15 of the 35. As the date grew closer, I kept getting calls—this person couldn't make it, then that person couldn't make it. Until, finally, it was just me and one other guy. I kept thinking, *What happened to everybody? I have a fear of heights, but I'm going skydiving, darn it.* I guess when it gets that high up, most people have a fear of heights.

So this guy and I go skydiving. We're on the plane with a random group of people. The plane takes off. An interesting thing: Although I have a fear of heights, I don't have a fear of flying. I don't know why. I've mentioned that emotions aren't logical. Fear is not logical. Knowing why you're afraid doesn't really matter. Knowing why is the booby prize; getting free of the fear is the real prize. People spend lots of time trying to analyze their fears and worries, but if we can be free of them, isn't that really what we're after?

When we approached jumping altitude, we all stood up. They opened the door for us to start jumping out. We were tandem-jumping, so one of the instructors and I were strapped together. We were the last in line. Two by two, the others walked up to the door and disappeared. I didn't know what was happening to them, how they were doing, or if their chutes opened. I thought, *What if I don't go?* But I had to. I stood there, stuck to the instructor, totally freaked out: *How do I stay on the plane? I don't want to go out that door. I don't know what's going to happen out there.*

As the line moved forward, my instructor and I scooched up until everyone else had jumped, and it was our turn. The instructor said, "All right, we're going to go on three. One, two—" and before he got to three, he pushed me out the door. No time for me to resist.

There I was, falling through the sky at 60 miles per hour, the ground below far away. Somebody was screaming. It wasn't me. I was in too much shock to scream. Since I was the student, I was supposed to pull the ripcord. I was also supposed to check my altimeter to know when it was time—at about 5,000 feet.

"Hey, check your altimeter," the instructor shouted.

"Oh, yeah, okay." I looked at my altimeter, going through the motions that they taught me an hour ago on the ground but not really seeing what our altitude was.

We continued falling.

"Check it again!"

I checked it again. Yikes! We were at 5,000 feet! Heart racing, I yanked the ripcord. The chute opened, and all I could think was, *Thank God. I'm alive. Thank God, I'm alive. For now.*

I felt such relief that the chute had opened. I've heard stories of people's chutes not opening. You know it can happen, right? If you have a fear of something happening, all you need to stoke that fear is to know it's happened or could conceivably happen. My fear was stoked. Believe me.

I took a breath, looked around, and wow! I felt such peace. *I'm alive.* It was so beautiful up that high. We were so high that it somehow wasn't freaky yet. I had these 10 seconds—maybe 20—of *Wow, this is so beautiful.*

Then things got real. The ground was getting a lot closer real fast. I could make out people and trees and buildings that, with luck, we wouldn't hit. We were coming in for a landing. We zoomed in, and we landed. On our feet. Safe. *Alive.* I felt so happy to be alive.

When I got home, I lay on the bed for a minute, and passed out. Massive shock to my reality. I'd done something that felt really scary to me. I wasn't cured, but I'd done it. I'd taken a step. And to me, at that point, I was okay with that. I felt like, if I could do something that scary, then I could do anything. No fears could ever stand in my way.

CLIMBING FROM A PLACE OF PEACE

There's a difference between overcoming fear and eliminating it. By skydiving, I overcame my fear. I beat it. But what I really wanted was to be over it. To be able to be up really high and feel peaceful.

I went parasailing with Chelsa and my two eldest daughters. Parasailing is when you're on a boat and you get hooked up to a parachute and the wind carries you high up in the air between 800 and 1,200 feet. We were all on the boat and we'd already paid for all of us, but I was going to skip my turn. I knew I could get myself to go up, but I also knew it wouldn't be fun for me. Chelsa and the girls all went up together. When they got back down, the girls said, "I want to go again!" They asked if they could go up with me this time. The captain of the boat, noticing I was going to skip out, said, "Yes, they can go again, and you won't have to pay for their second turn." Now, how could I say no to my little cuties? So I went up with them and they had a blast, but I didn't. They didn't know it, but inside, I was terrified. And that day, I decided, *You know what? I do want to let this go. I want to be able to have these experiences with my girls. I almost didn't go because I knew I wasn't going to like it. But now I'm going to keep putting myself in situations that involve heights so I can keep working through it until I'm at peace being up high.*

One of my friends suggested I join a rock climbing gym that he went to. When I first got there, I looked up at the wall—about 25 feet. I climbed two-thirds of the way up and thought, *Okay, that's good enough,* then climbed back down. I could have made it to the top, but I wanted to get comfortable being up high, so I decided to allow myself to ease into it. After a few more tries, I made it to the top. And I found that I really loved rock climbing. I've been going twice a week with my climbing friends and my wife ever since. I enjoy that it's physically challenging, and that it's mentally challenging, because you have to figure out the best approach to successfully climb each different route to the top. Some of the climbs are on a 55-foot wall. After a few months of super-high climbs, I got to the top, looked around, and realized I felt such a sense of peace, even though I was 55 feet in the air. The combination of repetition, Peace Process, and Instant Miracle finally paid off.

I'm sharing this story with you because I want to let you know that it's very rare for there to be fears that could take this much work to get through, but it's amazing when you do, and it's worth it. Peace is inevitable. Not only can we overcome a fear by having the courage to face it, but we can also transcend our fears so we feel just peace, love, joy, or simply a neutral feeling. Having broken through so many of my inner blocks over the years, including a few that took a long time to let go of, I'm confident these tools are going to help you get through anything.

Peace is inevitable in any situation if you want it. There isn't a situation where you can't get to peace—a past hurt, a past heartbreak, a current upset, physical fears. As long as you're willing to do the work and surrender to the fear, you'll get there.

CHAPTER 7

ROCK, TAFFY, WATER

I want to let you in on my best secrets for being more persuasive and influential in the world.

If you want to change your life in any of these ways . . .

- Get rich
- Do what you love for a living
- Lose weight
- Get healthy
- Find love
- Improve your sex life
- Connect with spirit
- Deepen your connection to God
- Or make any other change you want

. . . you need to loosen up. Don't be like rock or like taffy. Be like water. Let me explain. Some people believe the world is hard, set in stone. They live in a world that's like rock: "People don't change." "Things don't change." "This is the way things are." "This is reality." "This is just the way it is." "This is the way it's always been." "This is the way it's always going to be." Life is "fixed" and "stuck." This is the world of rock.

You may know some people like that, people who are rock-solid in their belief that success is impossible for them, or that it might be possible only for those who cheat or cheat the system. But if you want to be persuasive in the world, if you want to change the world, if you want to change your life, don't live in the world of rock. You won't get very far, if anywhere at all. Lots of people live in this world. It's not a fun world to live in. In reality, we all live in the world of rock some of the time. The goal is to spend as little time there as possible.

A step up from the world of rock is the world of taffy. Things move slowly here, but at least they move. Things can change. People can change. Life can change. The world can change, but it's hard. It's slow. It takes a lot of work. You can get what you want. It's possible, but it can be really hard, and it can take a really long time, and it also might not happen. Success is possible, but getting there can be a long, difficult, slow road.

Then there's the world of water. In this world, people can change. People *will* change. In fact, everyone is going to change. They may not change the way you want them to, but everyone will change. Some more than others, some faster than others, but everyone changes. *Everything* changes, and you can get everything you want. Everything is possible.

If water runs into a rock, does water say, "Oh, darn, I guess I have to give up. It's over. There's a rock in the way"? No. Water will either whoosh right around the rock, erode it, or find another path, but water goes where it needs to. Water can move fast. It can be a raging rapid, or it can be a still, calm pond. Water is intuitive. Water is flexible. Water will change its shape to fit the container. When you live in the world of water, life is more fluid and flexible. People naturally want to help you out. They're willing to change their minds about things. The world is flexible, and you can get what you want, sometimes a lot faster than you can imagine. In this world, success is highly likely, maybe even inevitable. Life is filled with miracles and can change in an instant. Tune in and be ready.

EXPECT THE BEST

How do you get from the world of rock or taffy to the world of water? You decide to do it. You change your perspective. How you see the world is how the world responds to you. If you see things as slow and people as inflexible, they will be. If you see that people want to help you and give you what you want, they often will.

What we expect is often exactly what we get. If you think things can't change, then why would you even bother to try? If you don't try, what do you think will happen? That's right: nothing. You fulfill your own expectation. And if you do that over and over, life slows down more and more. On the other hand, if you expect that things will flow and go your way, they often will. Making the transition from rock or taffy to water could be one of the most important decisions you ever make. I hope you make it right now by saying to yourself, "I see the world as water. I see people as water. I see myself as water."

The best way to move from rock to taffy to water is to surrender your attachment to a specific outcome. Stop being so rigid in the way you think things are, the way you think things need to be, and the way the things that you want to have in your life show up. We can all become fixated on things looking a certain way, but we can move out of that fixation if we just keep surrendering and surrendering and listening to our inner guidance.

One of the best ways to tune in is to just be present and get out of your mind. In any situation, the mind can always race around trying to figure things out, but the mind isn't where intuition, or guidance, usually comes from. It usually comes from a higher place. To access that guidance, getting centered and present is key. Some people meditate. Some listen to soothing music. I find it valuable to focus on something I find beautiful—a flower, a plant, a picture, a person, a book, a song—and become present with it, notice and appreciate its beauty, without categorizing or commentary. Just notice. Because when you're in that state of being present, it's usually easier to hear your intuition—to see, feel, and know.

BE PERSUADABLE

When you're in the world of water, you're persuadable, you're open to other ways of thinking, and to expansion. To get to that fluid place, you need to let go of the need to be "right." Needing to be right has probably killed more relationships than just about anything else. If you go into a discussion convinced you're right and the other person is wrong, and you're determined to *prove* that you're right, what are the chances of persuading them? Pretty close to zero. Maybe if you have amazing persuasion skills, you could do it. But the key is, if you want to be able to influence others, be influenceable. If you want to persuade others, first and foremost be persuadable.

Try being open-minded. Don't assume you're right. Look for the value in what other people might be saying. Where are they coming from? Even if you don't agree with them, look for how you *could* agree. What could you respect about their opinion? What could you appreciate about their perspective? What truth can you find in their perspective? Don't try to prove other people wrong. In fact, try to prove them right. Ask yourself, in what ways might they be right?

When you're in a discussion, you also want to notice the place you're coming from. Are you in rock mode? Are you unwilling to see that person's perspective? Or anyone's perspective, for that matter? Do others need to be wrong for you to be right? Or worse, if they're right, will that make you wrong? Coming from this rigid place

71

is very different from seeing other people as whole and complete and having truth in their point of view.

CELEBRATE BEING WRONG

It's totally okay to be wrong. In fact, I don't fear it, I celebrate it. Being wrong means I just learned something, and, at the same time, I get to let go of an idea that I believed to be true but wasn't. It's like removing "buggy" code from a computer program. You don't want to be attached to buggy code just because it's the code you've been using for years and your whole family uses it too. You don't want to stick with bad code just because it's yours. In the same way, you want to let go of the need to be right.

At my events and in my programs, I often talk about how I just want the best ideas in my mind I can get. In a team meeting, when we're looking for a creative solution, it doesn't matter if the winning idea is mine or a member of my team's, as long as it's the best idea. It doesn't matter if it's a new idea or an old one. I don't want to keep doing something because I've always done it. And I don't want to abandon something because something else is new. I'm not attached to being right. In fact, I'll celebrate being wrong because being wrong means two things: (1) I'm learning something new, and (2) I had an idea that wasn't true. Not only am I bringing in something good by learning something new, I'm getting something bad out.

I didn't always feel that way. When I was a kid, before we had search engines to look up information, my brother and I were always arguing about something or other. Back then, if you wanted information, you had to go to the library, and even then, who knew if we'd find the information we needed? If my brother and I had had the Internet, we could have settled those arguments quickly. But we didn't, and our arguments could last for days, each of us holding fast to our convictions, determined to be the one who was right. Now, you just look up what you need to know, and if you're wrong, you find out right away. The Internet has provided me with great opportunities to practice humility.

Most people have a hard time admitting when they're wrong, or apologizing for it. Not me. For the most part, I'm very comfortable with being wrong. There are exceptions, of course, times when I'm a little more attached or when my ego gets involved. But for the most part, I'm excited to learn, and I have no problem apologizing. I'm always aiming to surrender that part of my ego that needs to be right. When you let go of the ego, the attachment to an idea or way of being, to the part of you that wants to be right, imagine what you can let in. If you can be present to the feeling of being wrong, using the Peace Process will be a huge help with surrendering pieces of the ego and letting go of the smaller version of you to let the bigger, more divine version come out to play.

The need to be right or the feeling we've been wronged, our rigidity about a belief or fixation on an idea, not only gets in the way of expanding our knowledge and our lives, it can take a toll on us physically. Maybe we feel as though we've been wronged in some way: "They shouldn't have done this. This was wrong. They were wrong. They're bad." We're judging. We're locked into a belief system that can manifest as pain in our bodies, and there's growing proof that our thoughts and emotions contribute to all sorts of physical challenges.

I've seen people suffering from hearing loss because they weren't willing to hear something they needed to hear, or troubled with vision problems because they weren't willing to see something that they needed to see. I've seen these people let go of these fears and emotions and regain full use of their senses. I've witnessed people bent over with back problems from holding on to burdens they couldn't let go of, stand up straight and pain-free once they let that burden go. These are miracles.

Not long ago, I was working with a man at one of my events who felt really stressed about not having enough time. He'd taken the Time Abundance Assessment and scored 1.8 out of 10, so he had opportunities for growth. He came up onstage, sat on the stool, and told me he'd had back pain for the past 20 years. We started with the Peace Process. After a while, he started shifting around on his stool.

"These stools aren't the most comfortable," I said.

"No," he agreed, "but actually, my back is feeling pretty good."

As I was helping him release his stuck energy and his feelings about not having enough time, his back improved. By the time we finished and he stood up, not only did he feel dramatically more time-abundant, he said his back felt better than it had in 20 years.

BE A GOOD PERSUADER

Finally, be a good persuader. The key to being a good persuader is just to assume that everyone wants to help you get what you want. Just assume it. Even though it's not true, believe it anyway, because while *all* beliefs are limiting, this belief is much better than thinking, *Well, some people want to help me, but most people don't. Why would anybody want to help me? I have to do this all by myself.*

Let me stop a minute to explain what I mean by "all beliefs are limiting beliefs." All beliefs are limiting because they're definitive statements. That said, it's much better to have positive, empowering beliefs than negative ones. For example, thinking you're stupid is a negative limiting belief. On the other hand, thinking you're smart, while far better than thinking you're stupid, is also limiting, because you may think you know more than someone else. Or you may over-rely on your intellect to the exclusion of your gut instincts and intuition. The chapter titles in this book are what I call "divine beliefs." Believing success is inevitable is much more powerful than believing it's impossible—you're much more liable to just go for it, stick with it, knowing you'll get there eventually.

It's much more empowering to believe "we have all the time in the world" than to believe "there's not enough time in the day" or "there aren't enough days in the week." Do we have all the time in the world? That one's a paradox. We have only so many years to live. We don't know how long that is, but it's finite. But we have 24 hours in a day, 7 days in a week, 52 weeks in a year, and when you think of it that way—time stretches. Or if you watch the second hand on a stopwatch for 60 seconds, that minute can seem to go on forever.

Wayne Dyer said, "Loving people live in a loving world. Hostile people live in a hostile world. Same world." I believe most people are friendly. While that's a limiting belief, it's a positive one. I assume everybody is a loving person, even if they're not showing it in the moment. Deep down, everyone is loving, everyone is friendly, everyone wants to help you get what you want.

Operate and live in that world because what happens in your inner world creates your outer world. If you look for the best in people, you'll quite often find it. But if you look for the worst in people, you might also find it. And people tend to raise themselves up to the expectations of the people around them.

If you're always feeling that people aren't appreciating you, you'll always attract people not appreciating you. You'll always be seeking appreciation, and it will always show up as not enough appreciation, not enough respect, not enough whatever. Even when appreciation is being heaped on you like crazy, you won't absorb it. You won't notice it. You won't appreciate that you're being appreciated.

When I started enjoying a lot of success in my business, I felt like many of my peers who were equally successful or more so weren't appreciating or recognizing me. Deep down, I just wanted them to like me. And because I felt they didn't recognize and appreciate me, I felt they weren't appreciating Instant Miracle and the Peace Process. Which felt awful, because I wanted my friends to appreciate these techniques and the tools I use. My neediness for that recognition and appreciation was creating a lack of recognition and appreciation. As soon as I let my need go, suddenly people were saying, "Hey, tell me more about this. Hey, can you help me heal this stuff with Instant Miracle?" Out of the blue, friends started texting me, gushing with gratitude for how I'd impacted their lives.

I've seen the same things happen with clients who are in relationships. Maybe a wife is needy for attention from her husband. They work through that neediness, and suddenly, the husband is like an entirely different husband; he's overflowing with appreciation and attention and affection. The husband changed, but the husband didn't do anything. The wife changed, and by her changing, he changed. That's how it works. That's how your inner world creates your outer world.

I've seen similar results with people's financial situations, my own included. When you think, "I don't have enough, I don't have enough, I don't have enough," you're going to keep creating a world where you don't have enough. If you get into a place of "I've got so much, I've got so much, I've got so much," you're going to attract so much more. When you appreciate what you have ("Thank God, I'm rich!"), you're going to feel better instantly, and even more blessings will come into your life.

So be like water. This one shift in perspective is going to speed up getting what you desire in the game of life. Be on the lookout for new opportunities, new friends, and new challenges that could move your life in a positive new direction. Let yourself be guided by the powerful life force or God force that is your intuition. Tune in to the energy of life and see where it takes you.

CHAPTER 8

BLAME OUR PARENTS

Being a parent today is challenging enough. Can you imagine how hard it must have been for "cave parents"? We all evolved from cave parents. Back then, nearly all of the focus was on survival. Pretty much no attention was aimed at raising emotionally mature, healthy, happy, well-adjusted kids. Children can push any parent's buttons at times, but can you imagine what it was like for cave parents? Their frustration level must have been through the roof.

They didn't have running water, bathrooms, or washing machines. No microwave or nearby grocery store, or even words to communicate with. Plus, big scary things were trying to eat them every day. They spent most of their time trying to find food to survive another day. No diapers. Their constant worry was that you might start crying, which could attract the attention of animals that wanted to eat you. How much of those cave parents' fear, frustration, and anger turned into doing whatever they could to keep their kids quiet? In an ultra-high-stress environment, how often did they lash out at each other and their kids? Flash forward to our modern age. Most people have cars, houses, indoor plumbing, grocery stores, and more free time. And still, in today's environment, parenthood can be ultrahigh stress.

Chelsa and I have help around the house, and my wife's mom helps with the kids three days a week. Despite all this support, it's still challenging. We have to wake the girls up in the morning, get them dressed, brush their teeth. We need to make them breakfast, get them to actually eat breakfast, pack them in the car, drive them to school. Pick them up after school. Spend quality time together. Put them to bed at night. And we haven't even hit the homework phase yet! As I'm writing out what our day looks like with the girls, it doesn't sound all that tough. But if you have kids, you probably know that any one of these tasks can be a nightmare: "I don't want to get dressed!" "I don't want to go to sleep!" "Whaaaa! She took my toy!!!"

When our oldest child, Nala, was born, she had colic. For the first four months of her life, she cried all the time. At night, she'd cry for four hours straight before falling asleep. Chelsa and I tried everything to calm her down, but nothing worked. We saw doctors, healers. Nothing helped. I remember Chelsa waking up to Nala's crying after just getting to sleep, and she just looked so frustrated. I thought, "Uh-oh, please don't murder our baby!" Of course, she'd never harm our kids, but the stress can be so intense.

LOOK AT ME

The first cave parents didn't even have time to be super loving to their kids. Many kids didn't survive. Parents were very young and didn't live long enough to pass on much sage advice: "Watch out for saber-toothed tigers and poisonous berries. Oranges and fish make for good eats. Here's how to make a fire. Good luck, kid."

Mom and Dad didn't have time to play with their kids, let alone worry about their emotional well-being. If the kids were left alone in the cave, did they feel abandoned? Probably. If Mom and Dad were trying to find food instead of spending time with them, did they feel rejected? I'm guessing they did. Think about how many times kids say, "Look at me, look at me." Kids naturally want attention, pretty much all day, but parents have things to do. And in the caveman days, they had even more than we do.

It's a miracle we survived as a species. But survival was the game, and since you're reading this, your ancestors were some of the lucky ones who survived long enough to have kids who survived and had kids of their own, and so on down the generations to you. They won the survival game, but they lost the game of "raising emotionally healthy and well-adjusted kids." They lost because they weren't playing that game. They couldn't. Eventually, we moved from caves to huts and on to houses. We moved from hunting and gathering, to farming and grazing, to shopping and cooking. Demands on parents have been huge all along, but we live longer, with more support and fewer dangers.

Kids today can get more attention, though still not enough to meet their infinite desire for it. When we had just one kid, I realized that even if Chelsa and I dedicated every minute of our day to our child, it wouldn't fill the vast need for attention that's inside every new person. And for families who have two or three kids (as we do now), and a job, and any interests of your own, you're toast.

As young kids growing up, if Mom is on the phone, cooking dinner, or tending to a sibling, we can still feel abandoned, rejected, or not "good enough." Yet we're infinitely powerful, infinitely creative, and infinitely resourceful. And as little children who don't know any better, we can put that infinite power toward feeling infinitely insecure.

As babies, we get an enormous amount of natural attention just for being born. As we grow older, we have to earn that attention: "Look at me" (and see me do something that you'll give me attention for). "Look at me" (and smile and laugh the way you did when I said anything you thought was funny). "Look at me" (and love me the way you did when I didn't have to do anything for love and attention). And we get skewed ideas about how to get that attention.

One day, Nala, Zoey, and I were swimming in the pool. I was holding them in my arms, when suddenly Nala took off—she just swam away. I called after her to come back to our hug, and then I turned to Zoey and said, "At least I still have my Zoey."

"Oh, no, you don't have me," she said, and then pushed me away and swam off. I realized that, in her mind, she'd seen my chasing Nala as her sister getting more love and attention. So, in her mind, Zoey reasoned that to be loved, you need to be pursued, and she couldn't just give or get free, easy love for nothing.

No matter what our circumstances, we get all kinds of crazy ideas we need to untangle. As I said in the first chapter, our interpretation of any given event shapes our reality, and if we attach the wrong meaning to that event, it can mess us up.

WE'RE ALL SCREWED UP

The point is, we can't *not* mess up our kids. And there's absolutely nothing our parents could have done to keep us from having made these connections, misunderstandings, and different interpretations that we may be blaming on our parents, feeling they didn't give us the attention or love that maybe our friends or siblings got. No matter how healthy your background, no matter how healthy you are now, you're going to have some of these misconceptions. You're going to be a bit screwed up about a few things. We're all screwed up to some degree, and that's just the way it is. We should feel no shame about being a little (or a lot) crazy and wanting to clean up some of the misconceptions and the pains that go with them.

It's my intention that this book will help you untwist and untangle the misinterpretations that could be keeping you stuck or suffering. Some of us had better parents, some worse. But whichever parents we got, our parents probably had it even worse than we did. Every generation's parents are better than the generation's before to some degree, because, hopefully, we learn from that previous generation. I'm sure there are exceptions, but overall, parents are getting better and better.

We all grow up and develop doubts, fears, insecurities, and limiting ways of thinking. Many of these patterns develop naturally as we grow up. Many of them we learn through osmosis—just by being around our parents, who were raised by parents one generation closer to the caveman era than we are. Here's the bottom line: we're living our lives based on a lineage of emotionally screwed-up people who were doing the best they could to keep us alive and, hopefully, not mess us up as much as their parents messed them up.

Think about how ideas change or shift from one generation to the next. When I grew up, the concept of hitting your child being "child abuse" had just become a "thing." Before that, hitting your child with your hand or a belt was considered "good child-rearing." Right now, "bullying" is a big deal. When I grew up, it was just a way of life for many kids—including me.

I would ride the bus to school sick to my stomach almost every day, afraid of what might happen. Sometimes I'd get punched in the back of the head for no reason. Other times I'd just get teased about my beat-up old clothes, or my nerdy glasses that were held together with tape. To avoid the abuse, I'd try to make myself invisible. I'd slink down in my seat and avoid eye contact, looking down at my notebook or outside if I had a window seat.

One time, I rode my older brother's ancient bike, which was way too big for me, to a 7-Eleven store. I was wearing an ugly sweater, my taped-up glasses, and bell-bottom jeans. I'd just laid my bike on the pavement when this really cute, well-dressed girl about my age, maybe a year or so older, walked out. She looked straight at me and said hi. I was like, *Whoa. This pretty girl is talking to me.* I thought maybe she needed directions or something, and I had a flash of hope that maybe she was interested in me. Instead, out of nowhere, she started making fun of everything about me: my pants, my sweater, my glasses, my bike; and I got all defensive about them. "Well, it's my brother's bike. I broke my glasses, and we don't have any money."

Her comments stung because she said what I was already thinking about myself. Her comments pushed the buttons in me that were already there. If only I'd known the Peace Process when I was a kid. I could have let so much of my shame and self-judgment go and had a lot more confidence when I was in school.

Growing up, I didn't realize that teasing could be playful and lighthearted. I always took it as people making fun of me. It felt mean and like people were trying to start a fight, which I had too much of at home. Plus, because I was so sensitive, when people teased me, I took it personally. What could have been playful teasing I interpreted as, *They don't like me*, which made me wonder, *What's wrong with me?* Maybe they were playing around, I don't know. It didn't matter. I felt they were being mean. And I refused to be mean back or to tease back. I saw enough people in pain at home. I didn't want to cause pain to anyone else. I know that girl let out her venom on me because she'd probably gotten plenty of it at home herself and she was just acting out of her own insecurities. All bullies are first bullied themselves. They deserve love and compassion too.

If you were abused as a child or suffered serious pain, I want to tell you: You can let it go. You can get to peace about it. You can forgive the people who hurt you. Not because they deserve it, but because you deserve the peace. You can forgive yourself if you need to. You can let go of any shame. I believe if I'd had a different attitude as a kid, if I'd had more confidence back then, I could have seen things differently. Sometimes I could have teased back playfully. I probably would have stood up for myself more. Plus, those horrible glasses? If I'd had a lot of confidence back then, I'd have *rocked* those glasses.

In my experiences with thousands of people from all over the world, I've witnessed miracle after miracle after miracle of people healing so many different things. That's not to say it's going to be a piece of cake. The processes go deep and sometimes can be really challenging, but I believe we can get to peace about anything. I believe that peace is inevitable if we're willing to do the work. If we're willing to feel the feelings, if we're willing to do the Peace Process, then getting to peace is inevitable.

In this book, I've given you the tools to get started. They work. I also highly recommend you come to one of our Instant Miracle live events, or you could work with one of the coaches from my team. I think we can help anyone get to a place of peace about anything. I haven't seen anything that works as quickly or effectively as the Peace Process and Instant Miracle. Plus, when we use the tools in this book, we're untangling the threads of all the messed-up stuff from the earliest days of humanity, and coaxing the knots out.

THE GIFT AND THE PRICE

If we don't work on these stories from our past, they continue to shape us as adults. When I was in my early twenties, I started my own business—Giftastic—selling gift cards, but I wasn't putting much energy into it. I was afraid of taking the steps I needed to take to make it a success—cold-calling was a big one. I also had a full-time job in manufacturing, which I didn't like at all and didn't feel I was very good at. I felt lost and unmotivated. Every day I spent in that job, a small part of me died inside.

As time progressed and I became more discouraged about the job and my business, I started feeling weak emotionally and, eventually, after a year with the company, I attracted the attention of the company bully, Charles. He was a like a shark who could smell blood in the water. He'd never messed with me until one day, when I was feeling at my weakest, Charles made an *L* with his thumb and index finger, held it up to his forehead, and called me a loser in front of everyone at work. I felt such shame and embarrassment. One time was bad enough. But he held that *L* up to his forehead every single day—in front of my co-workers, in front of a girl I liked, in front of my boss. I didn't know what to say or do.

I was so miserable that I knew I had to get the heck out of there. The pain of being at work with Charles was worse than the pain of doing the things I was frightened of doing to make my business successful. I had to make my business work. So I hired my first success coach to help me, and I started taking action. Every day, consistently, I took care of the tasks I needed to for my business to succeed. I worked at my job from nine to five and on my gift-card business in the evening and on weekends. I started getting stronger on the inside again. And then, one day, Charles, perhaps sensing my inner strength, simply stopped harassing me. Once again, when you change inside, the outer world also changes.

If I'd stayed stuck in the story of how painful my job was, and stayed immersed in my insecurities about my ability to succeed, I might never have gotten out. We've all been through tough stuff, some more than others, but we don't have to be owned by the story. Everything that happens to us has a gift and a price. Charles's bullying was extremely painful. The gift was that I felt so terrible, I was forced to do something about my life. I ended up quitting my job, working for myself, and eventually becoming a success coach myself. Charles's motivating me to follow through on this path has led me to some of my greatest success and happiness.

The gift was well worth the price of the pain, but I don't need to continue paying the price forever. I don't need to be angry with Charles. I don't need to be upset about what happened. I don't need to see myself as a victim. I let all of that go. It's just an event that occurred in time, but if we don't let go and we carry it with us, it messes up our life, we keep paying a price, and we may never get the gift.

Many years ago, when my friend Sean introduced me to the idea of everything in life having a gift and a price, I debated with him about the accuracy of that concept. *Do gifts have a price?* I wondered. *Does gratitude?* Now, I don't need anything to be undeniably true to find the value in it. Even if not "everything" has a gift and a price, I believe all our suffering has a gift inside. Like the pearl in an oyster that results from a grain of sand slipping inside and irritating it for most of its life, there's a rare and precious gift in any part of your life that has caused you pain.

Part of the reason my mom divorced my dad was because of all the fights they had. Another part of the reason was that my dad was tough on us kids. I don't need to go into detail here about his being tough on the kids. I'll just say my mom wanted to spare me that. (Later, after a few of her relationships didn't work out and my dad mellowed out, I think my mom may have regretted her decision.) But something happened the day the police came to make sure my dad left the house peacefully, when the marriage was legally over. My dad cried. I'd never seen him cry, and it made me cry. Our eyes met, and in that moment we formed a special bond. He realized someone in our house loved him. And from then on, he was kinder and gentler with me than with anyone else.

The fights between my parents weren't really about money. They may not have realized it at the time, but underneath, those fights about how to spend or save were about love and safety. My dad wanted love. And my mom wanted safety. It makes sense. First, they both had different core beliefs about money. Both my parents' fathers passed away when my parents were young. They both grew up in tough financial circumstances. My mom learned, "We need to be very careful because we could run out of money." She believed this could happen at any time—especially if my dad were to die young, as both of their fathers had. My dad learned that "no matter what happens with money, we'll be okay." There's always a way to hustle to make extra money, or a friend who will help out. So my mom never felt safe financially while my dad always felt safe.

And then there was love. Or what felt like the lack of it. Since both my parents' dads died when they were young, neither of them got much love growing up from their one remaining parent, who had a lot to deal with besides just raising kids. My mom's mom became an alcoholic and drank all day, every day. My dad's mom remarried into a family that already had two kids and treated my dad like an outsider. When two people feel that they aren't getting the love they need, and they have two different core needs, it can cause a lot of problems. In my parents' case, they split up.

When we leave one relationship, we often attract another one that's very similar, because we attract what we most need to push our buttons, so we can work through those issues. What starts as a whisper on the wind turns into a loud knock at the door, and, eventually, a force that knocks down the house. Until we get it. Until we work through those issues. It's set up this way by God, the universe, our intuition, whatever mysterious forces run the universe.

If you want to attract different people and different situations into your life, you need to let go of your hot buttons or triggers. Remember, we attract into our lives what we most desire and what we most fear, or watered-down versions of the two. I mentioned that my mom's first relationship after the divorce was just as tumultuous as her relationship with my dad, maybe even more so. And many of her financial fears she fought so hard about with my dad came to pass. She attracted what she needed to attract so that she would feel what she needed to feel in order to heal what she needed to heal. Some of which may have been fully healed and some of which probably still could use some work.

The work is never complete for any of us. There's always an infinite number of things we can work on in ourselves in order to heal. I'm always working on myself, and healing and releasing whatever comes up for me or whatever old patterns I notice that no longer serve me. And even though I've healed thousands of my own challenges, there are always new ones—some that I take upon myself and others that are thrust into my life— that require more work to transcend.

I came to realize that one of the greatest gifts of my parents' divorce was that I got to have a great relationship with my dad, which may not have happened any other way. And because of how our visitation was set up, I had dates with my dad once a week. Sometimes my older sister came too, but most of the time, it was just the two of us. None of the other kids in my family had that privilege.

There are always gifts in the hard parts of our lives—if we look for them. Most people can't see the gifts because they're too caught up in the story of how they were wronged. You can be wronged and still find a gift. Maybe in certain situations you were a victim. But as long as you hold on to the story, you'll keep suffering. And even if you can find the gifts and the blessings, if you're still in pain when you look back at that event that happened, then you're still paying the price.

You don't need to pay the price. I believe you can get to neutral or peace about any situation in life. You can let go of the pain, the hurt, the resentment, the anger, and get to peace with it.

That doesn't mean what happened is acceptable. If you were mistreated, you don't want to keep allowing that. But it does mean that you can find acceptance with the historical fact that it took place in your life. You can forgive. You can let go, and let it go, and move on without carrying the weight of that experience around with you.

Take the wisdom. Take the learning. Take the strength. Take the richness and depth of your heart, your spirit, and your compassion. And leave behind the bitterness, the anger, the shame, the guilt, and the sadness. It's time to move on with new freedom, with new tools, new power, remembering who you are. You are a piece of the divine. Its power flows through you. The same power that created the entire universe flows through you. You can have, you can be, and you can do anything your gigantic heart desires.

What's beautiful is that it doesn't matter what happened; all we have to do is stay out of our minds and stay in our bodies. Just keep feeling whatever feelings come up without trying to make them go away, without trying to analyze them, without judging them. Just letting those feelings fully and completely be there. Keep our attention on the most intense part, and keep sending it love.

Everything in life is a gift. Every pain has a gift. Everything that has gone "wrong" in your life, or that your parents didn't get right, was all for a greater good—if you're willing to look for the gifts and let go of the story that keeps you paying the price.

Yes, our parents may have "screwed us up," but it was impossible not to. They also survived and helped us survive. As long as we're blaming them, let's be sure to also blame them and all our ancestors for helping us not only survive, but get to a place in our evolution where we have the luxury of being able to move beyond the game of *surviving,* so we can play a new game called *thriving,* where we can make our lives an incredibly rich and rewarding adventure. You have the power to write your own new life story. A new chapter awaits you.

CHAPTER 9

YOU ARE LOVED, DEEPLY LOVED

We all want love. Maybe we want a relationship, the love of our friends, our family, our peers—bottom line, we want to be loved. Yet we often forget that the ultimate source of love is within us. The more love you feel for yourself, the more other people will naturally love you and gravitate toward you. The more attachments you have to being loved, the more neediness, the more you're going to be searching for that love out in the world, and it's always going to be elusive. But if you surrender those attachments or that neediness, love will be easy. Not that relationships necessarily will be easy, but love will be easy. You won't be fighting to get it, chasing it, pushing it away when you get it. It will be readily available. You'll be happy. You'll feel loved.

Years ago, I had a dream of what an amazing relationship could be like. I would see couples at seminars holding hands, cuddling, growing together, and I wanted a relationship like that, so I started dating, dating, dating, but nothing clicked. After many years of not finding a great relationship, I found myself feeling really lonely and ashamed I was single, as though maybe there were something wrong with me. Finally, when I started working with the tools of abundance in my business—Instant Miracle and Peace Process—I used them on myself to release my angst about feeling lonely and my shame about being single. Once I let all that angst and shame go, within a few months I met my wife. We've been together for more than 12 years and have three amazing little girls. One of the biggest joys of my life is my family life. When we started dating, and I was no longer needy for a relationship, ashamed, or fearful, when I felt much more centered and peaceful, my business and personal income started taking off as well. My health improved. I had more energy and a stronger immune system, and pain from a knee injury disappeared.

That's how abundance works. One area affects all areas. And love abundance, especially, impacts health, wealth, time—everything. You have massive control and massive influence over what you have and how much. But your emotional and energetic blocks, though able to be released, can restrict the amount of good stuff that flows into your life.

My wife and I had been doing this work on ourselves for years—releasing our blocks to love—but it wasn't until we both took the Love Abundance Assessment that we saw blocks we couldn't before. We could pinpoint specific areas where we weren't very abundant or where we needed more work to become even more abundant.

It turned out that of all the Abundance Assessments, my wife scored the lowest in Love Abundance. It broke my heart because I love her so much, everyone loves her so much, and yet, she wasn't experiencing all that love. When we found out her scores were low, we immediately started working to release those blocks and raise her scores. That work dramatically enhanced the quality of our relationship, and even more, the quality of her life in general, because those blocks to love were also affecting her relationships with her parents and friends.

THE FIVE RULES FOR SUCCESSFUL RELATIONSHIPS

To boost our Love Abundance Assessment scores, Chelsa and I adhere to these five steps for successful relationships. These rules, along with the Abundance tools, have helped improve our relationship as well as the relationships—both professional and personal—of thousands of people I've worked with around the world.

Rule #1: Make yourself happy first.
I've talked about the importance of a supportive environment—both internal and external. When you pay attention to those environments, you increase your level of happiness, which increases the happiness of those around you. How much easier is it for your partner to be happy when they're around somebody who's happy? In this case—you. And the reverse is true. I love it when my wife is happy. It makes me happy.

Rule #2: I'm upset because of me, not because of you.
I still blame my wife a lot of the time, but deep down, I know it's my stuff. I do come around. I work on it and heal myself. Or we help heal each other. Chelsa and I know it's not her fault I'm upset, and it's not my fault she's upset. It's *my* fault I'm upset, and it's *her* fault she's upset. It's easy to blame other people for our upsets, but the real healing comes when we take ownership of it. If someone I care about were to point their finger at me and yell, "You're a big purple monster," I'd laugh. I don't have a trigger about being a big purple monster. But if they told me no one will ever love me, I'm selfish, or I'm not smart, then that might get to me. The key is realizing it's not the other person who's upsetting me; it's me. The upset is somewhere deep inside, and that other person is just the catalyst that helps me to see that hot button so I can heal it.

One day not long ago, Chelsa's mom was babysitting for us. I thought she was babysitting that night too, and didn't realize we had only until six o'clock. After an afternoon running errands together, I had secretly planned a date night for us, and when I found out we needed to be home early, I was disappointed, and asked Chelsa to see if her mom could stay longer so we could go to a special new restaurant. I'd already made reservations, so we needed only an extra hour.

Chelsa knew her mom needed a break. She didn't want to inconvenience her mom and refused to ask for more time. This pushed a button in me that made me feel I wasn't important to her. If I were important, she would have asked her mom for extra time. I secretly felt mad at her for the rest of the night! Even though I was mad at her, underneath the anger, I was just hurt. I knew it was my stuff to work through, so I did, and we were back to cuddling before the night was over.

Rule #3: Be honest, even when it's hard.

It's tough to do. We don't want to rock the boat. I don't want to hurt someone's feelings. I don't want to feel the guilt for hurting their feelings. But if we hurt someone's feelings, often it's because we've hit one of their buttons, something they need to heal. We can't take responsibility for someone else's feelings. I want the truth in relationships. I remember Byron Katie saying, "Would you rather be happy, or do you want the truth?" I'll take the truth, and then I'll get myself happy. If the truth upsets me, that's my fault. That's my bad. That's an indicator that I have another level to grow to. So tell me the truth, and I'll tell you the truth.

Relationships are so much better when people tell each other the truth—it's cleaner and healing. I think we all want to be with someone who is open to honest communication, taking responsibility for their upsets and working through their stuff. It's so important to be honest, even though it's hard and the person you're coming clean with might be upset in the moment, because it builds trust and respect. It creates greater intimacy and a deeper and longer-lasting connection.

Possibly the toughest people to be honest with are people you work with. Maybe a member of your team is underperforming and you need to let them know. I have a woman on my team who's really good at project management, but when she first came on board, I had a gut feeling I shouldn't put her in charge of people. I felt she'd rub them the wrong way. For a long time, I kept my feelings to myself, because I didn't know how to tell her. Eventually, I shared my feelings. She was really upset, but we worked through it with the Peace Process and Instant Miracle.

Afterward, her awareness of how she was with other people was so much greater. She wasn't defensive. She looked at her people skills as another area that wasn't one of her strengths. But she also committed to developing in that area, took trainings, and discovered tools and techniques for working with people, to help them feel more comfortable with her. She was extremely valuable to the business with the skills she had before, and now she's one of the most important people on the team, if not *the* most important person.

While it's hard being honest when we think we'll hurt someone, it's also hard when we think that person's going to be angry. The thing is, if we're afraid they're going to be angry, we're likely to manifest that fear and bring anger out in them. But if you get to a place of peace about the fact they might get angry—or not—you can get to a place of neutrality.

Rule #4: Be respectful, even when you're mad.
I feel we should always treat the other person with respect, but sometimes we can't help doing otherwise. Sometimes you don't have any control. That button is being pushed. You want to say, "Ahhhh! You _____ !" So how do you remain respectful when you're angry? Let's say someone's cheated on you. Or maybe they lied to you. You want to be as respectful to the other person as you can, holding them in high regard, tuning in to their positive intent. If they're angry, it helps if you realize that when we're angry, it's because underneath the anger there's hurt. And they may not be aware of what's going on.

In his book *Love Is Letting Go of Fear*, Gerald Jampolsky says that communication is either an expression of love or an expression of fear, and expressing fear is really a cry for help. Normally these cries for help look like yelling, anger, or sadness. And when someone is yelling at you, the natural response for most people is to get defensive and yell back or get upset and cry. Basically, we answer a cry for help with another cry for help. But if you tune in to the other person's hurt and look for the positive intent in whatever they were doing, you can usually work through it, or at least come to a place of peace within yourself.

When you're feeling hurt or upset, if you can realize and own that it's your own upset regardless of what the other person did, you can work through it with the Peace Process. But in the heat of the moment, simply remember that this is somebody you love, somebody you care about. All situations can be resolved if both people are willing.

Here's a hypothetical situation to illustrate respectful communication. Let's say I offer to pick up Nala from school, and at the last minute I call Chelsa and say, "You know what? I can't pick up Nala from school. I need you to pick her up." Chelsa could go all supernova and yell, "I can't believe you'd do this. You said you were going to pick her up. Why aren't you? And why did you wait until the last minute to tell me? I can't believe you're leaving me in this situation. I have to wake Zoey and Lily from their naps, and Lily is going to be upset all day. You've ruined my day. I hate you!" And I could get all defensive and yell back at her, "Picking up the kids is your job! I was hoping I could help you out, but it didn't work out. You get to play with the kids all day. I have real problems to deal with!"

Following this path leads nowhere good. Instead of yelling, my wife could explain that I'm putting her in a tough situation and ask me what happened. Her underlying fear is that she's going to have a really hard time with the kids for the rest of the day since they won't get their nap. Maybe I can offer to help out more once I get home by putting all three girls to bed.

And I could explain that something critical came up at work and I can't leave early or my boss might fire me or an important project could fail. From that place, Chelsa can be more understanding.

A great tool I learned from a friend of mine many years ago is the three modes of communication. The modes are superior, peer-to-peer, and inferior. Superior mode is where people go to try to force their will. They believe if they go to superior mode, they're going to a stronger place. But superior mode is usually like a false sense of superiority, a sense of "I know better. This is the way it should be. Do what I say. Because I said so." When people are angry, they usually go to superior mode. If someone is in superior mode, it makes the other person want to go into superior mode to push back and hold their ground.

Peer-to-peer is communication between friends, a husband and wife, or co-workers. It's the mode of equals, and most conversation occurs at this level. But if you want to de-escalate a situation instead of escalating it, the fastest way is to go straight to inferior mode.

Here's an example from my business. A woman sent me an angry e-mail complaining about my marketing and saying how all of us marketers are just trying to sell our stuff and that we don't care about anyone. My wife read that e-mail and said, "Where does she live? I want to go kick her butt for saying mean things like that to you." My wife was in superior mode. I replied back to the e-mail and said, "I'm so sorry to hear that you aren't connecting with my marketing messages. I understand that it can feel like people don't care, but I actually do. That's why I'm taking the time to reply to your e-mail. I've often felt like it would be great if I could get people to join my life-changing programs without doing any marketing at all. But I don't know how to make that work. What I'm doing now seems to be working really well and creating lots of happy customers. But if you have ideas or suggestions for how to get customers in a different way, I'm all ears. Please share your thoughts and recommendations on what you think I could do differently to show I care and still get people into my programs."

With inferior-mode communication, instead of telling people what to do, you share what's happening with you, explain your reasoning, and then ask for input about a possible solution. When you do this, you take the wind out of their sails. They don't have anything to fight against, and everything tends to smooth over fairly quickly. And in the case of the angry e-mailer, she replied back to me with a big fat apology, purchased several of my programs, and became a raving fan.

Rule #5. Do your best with all the above.

We're human. We make mistakes. We get upset. We forget we really are divine, loving beings. We get hungry or hangry (hungry/angry) sometimes. We have a bad night's sleep. Something at work upsets us and we unconsciously take it out on the wrong person. Our partner gazes too long at an attractive person and pushes a button. We're insecure bundles of hot buttons just waiting to be triggered.

There's absolutely no way you won't become upset with your partner from time to time. You might even lash out and say or do things you would never do in a normal frame of mind. You've got to forgive yourself for being a human and making mistakes—that's what humans do. We're mistake-making machines. But if you're willing to learn from your mistakes and take responsibility for your upsets and your reactions, it makes for a much cleaner, happier relationship.

WHOSE LOVE ARE YOU SEEKING?

One thing we need to accept in our relationships is that people aren't going to show up exactly the way we'd like them to. Can you think of someone's love—or approval or respect—you've been trying to get all your life and they won't give it to you? In reality, they could be giving it to you, but they're not giving it to you in the way you want it. Of course, there's the chance that they're not giving it to you at all. We often push away what we're needy for. As sad as it is, your button about neediness could be pushing your parents' love away. Or your spouse's. Or your kids'.

I had a lot of neediness for my oldest daughter's love. I used to say, "Just let me cuddle you!" And she'd say, "No!" In *The 5 Love Languages*, Gary Chapman discusses the different ways we experience or receive love. My primary love language is physical touch. I'm a super-cuddlebug, and so is my wife. My middle daughter Zoey's love language is also physical touch. She loves to cuddle. When she started walking, she'd toddle over to the couch, and cuddle the couch!

Nala's love languages are spending quality time and receiving gifts. She feels loved when someone spends time with her and when someone buys her something. She cherishes the gift long after she's received it. If someone's given her a shirt, even if she's had it for a while, when she puts it on she'll remind us of who gave it to her. "Auntie Beso gave me this shirt," she might say, and she feels happy and filled with gratitude for her aunt.

That's awesome that she feels that way, but it was hard for me, because I wanted to cuddle. Then I realized I was wanting her to show up for me in a certain way, which was not how she gives or receives love. So I did some work, and I let that go (or most of it, anyway). And when I dropped that neediness, and let go of how I wanted her love to show up, she came around. As I changed, she changed. She's not going to completely switch love languages, but she likes to cuddle more now that I'm not trying to get, get, get. And if she hadn't come around, that would have been okay too.

DON'T LET THE FAIRNESS TRAP GET YOU

One of the biggest secrets to love abundance in any relationship is to give more. Give without worrying about what you'll get back. Don't worry that everything's 50-50 and fair. The desire to make things fair in the world is noble. But the need for things to be fair for us is a sickness, because our minds will always be on the lookout for how we might not be getting enough compared to other people.

My kids are very much into being fair. I teach them to be fair with others, but not to expect that things will be fair for you. Taking turns is fair. However, things can't always be fair. The girls are different ages, and they can't all get the same things. They can't all do the same things. Lily, our youngest, can't use an iPad, but Nala and Zoey can. Nala can read a book, but Zoey can't.

Sometimes, the whole idea of fairness can get out of hand. When we're playing around and I'm giving them each a turn to be thrown high into the air onto the pillow-covered bed, it's a lot of fun. But then there's the complaining, "You threw her higher! How come she got a longer turn than me? I want as good a turn as she had!" It gets crazy. And I end up saying, "If I hear that one more time, you'll get no turns! I'm going to throw you exactly the amount of times I want to throw you, exactly as high as I want to throw you. You know what? Sometimes it might be better than Zoey got, and sometimes it might not. That's just too bad. You can either enjoy our playtime together, or not. Trying to keep it fair is not fun for me, and I am not playing that game. I'm playing the game of I'm just having a great time with my girls. If you want to play that game, then let's play."

The need for fairness is a sickness. When you think everything is supposed to be fair, should be fair, and has to be fair, especially in relationships. You want to destroy your relationship? Try to make sure you're giving the same amount that you're getting from your partner: "Wait a second. I'm giving a little bit more than you are. It's time for you to give a little bit back." No. You out-give them. Have a competition for who can out-give each other. That's a recipe for a great relationship. It's a great recipe for a great friendship. It's a recipe for success in business because when your customers get way more than they paid for, they'll keep coming back for more. It's a great recipe for being an amazing human being.

Aim to be the most generous person that you can, without forgetting to be generous to yourself. It's not "give away and deplete yourself." Be strong, and give when you're strong. Give from strength and love. Don't worry about it being fair to you. Don't worry about things being fair to other people. Just give; you'll be amazed at how it will open your heart and how much more abundance flows into your life.

THE SEEDS OF LOVE ARE PLANTED BY OUR PARENTS

So much of how open or closed your heart is to love is a result of all that happened with your parents as you were growing up. To help open your heart, find a quiet place and imagine you were raised by totally perfect parents. They always loved you. They said and did everything you wished they would. And they never did anything you wished they hadn't done. Imagine how much you'd love these perfect parents that loved you so perfectly. Your parents are giving you all the time and attention you always wanted. They're playing with you and doing things with you that you always wished they'd done, being your best friend but also looking out for you. If you really take the time to imagine it, it feels so good, doesn't it? So open. So light. So free.

Now imagine that your heart stays wide open as you realize that even though your mother and father didn't say and do all those things that your idealized mother and father may have, it was because they were dealing with their own messed-up stuff from their own messed-up parents. And because parents—who have responsibilities in addition to your well-being—no matter how perfect, possess finite resources of time and energy to fulfill the infinite desire for attention that children have. It's time to forgive them and love them even more. In most cases our parents had it harder than we did. For the most part, our parents' generation was raised by less aware parents.

What if the truth is that your real mom and dad *were* your perfect mom and dad?

The ones you needed to grow the way you've grown, the ones who helped you to get stronger, be more compassionate, and learn the lessons you needed to learn to become the person you are today. The perfect human being God always hoped he was helping to create when you were born.

All the things that happened to me growing up got me here, so I could teach you, and all the things that happened to you got you here, so you can now learn to heal yourself and others and get on an even faster path to growth and achievement. There are so many gifts that came from your mom and dad being exactly the way they were—imperfectly perfect, as we all are—because we've all evolved from caveman and cavewoman parents, and we're barely starting to do a little better than that now.

Imagine loving your actual mom and dad the way you imagined you'd love your perfect mom and dad. It might not be completely possible, but imagine loving your real mom and dad without any of the hurt, anger, upsets, or resentments. Notice how great that feels.

You can forgive your mom and dad for whatever the heck they did or didn't do, for all the things that prompted you to build protective walls around your feelings and around your heart. You can let those walls go. You don't need protection anymore because you're trying to protect yourself from your feelings. You don't need to be protected from your feelings. You're powerful. You're strong. You can feel your feelings. You can feel your anger. You can feel your rejection, your shame. You can feel all of it. Whatever you need to feel, you're strong enough. And love your parents as much as you can—not for their sakes, but for your own—because the more you can love them, the more you can love yourself, your partner, your friends, and the world.

Even if your heart can't be completely wide open for your real parents yet, maybe it's open far wider than ever. And maybe, just maybe, it can be completely open. The same applies to others in your life. Your friends, for example. You actually had the perfect friends growing up. They may not have been what you think would have been perfect. But they were the ones to give you the lessons you most needed to become the person you're becoming.

Our ultimate power comes from working on ourselves, because when we work on ourselves, everyone else changes. Even somebody who treats everyone else the same way—maybe that person is dismissive, cold, or a bully—isn't going to be that way to you when you're different and you're healed and you're whole.

YOU ARE SO LOVED

I want to devote the rest of this chapter to letting you know how loved you are. You are so, so loved—that love is far greater than you'll probably ever know. You're so rich, and as you read this book, I hope you're realizing it more and more, and attracting more love every day. You are infinitely powerful. Your success is inevitable if you're willing to do the work, work on yourself, and stay with it. We've always had an unlimited supply of love available to us, streaming down and shining on us even though we didn't let it all in.

You can only experience the amount of love from the universe and from people you care about, in proportion to how much you're willing to give to yourself and accept for yourself. The entire universe is just trying to shower so much love in your life. We can freak out and feel like it's too much: *I don't know if I can handle that much love. I don't know if I can handle that much joy, that much success, and that much abundance.* Yes, you can. It might be scary, but let it in anyway. Let it in. Let yourself love yourself more and more every day.

Remember, all fears are fears of feelings, and if we can be with our feelings, have the courage to feel our feelings instead of stuffing them down, hiding them in the closet, or distracting ourselves, we can heal. Sure, we're all going to stuff our feelings and distract ourselves sometimes, and that's okay, but just realizing you're trying to run from the feeling is huge. When you realize you're trying to run, tell yourself, *I'm trying to run from this thing; let me work on this. I surrender. I'll find where the feeling is most intense. I'll be present to it. I'll send it love. I'll put down the remote. I'll put down the chocolate. I'll go downstairs. I'll open the closet door. I'll pick up the crying baby* [note that this baby is you]. *I'll nurture it. I'll love it. I'll rock it. I'll send it love. I'll soothe it.*

Soothe yourself. Cradle yourself. Love yourself. Respect yourself. Care about yourself. Take care of yourself. Forgive yourself. If you're never going to be perfect, you might as well give up. Give up the need to be perfect, and love yourself in all your imperfect glory. Love the unlovable parts of yourself. Love yourself even though sometimes you feel angry. Love yourself even though sometimes you feel ungrateful. Love yourself even though sometimes you feel weak or powerless.

Don't pile on the extra layers of *I feel weak and powerless. I'm so ashamed of being weak and powerless. I hate myself for being so shameful.* Hating hurt doesn't help. You are weak. It's okay. So am I. We all are. You're also strong. In fact, you're a badass, and you need to appreciate it more.

I'm an amazing husband in a lot of ways, and in some ways I'm not—and that's okay. I'm a package deal. If you want someone who's a gourmet cook or, hell, even a bad cook who likes to cook and at least cooks for you, you're going to have to find somebody else. I'm not that husband. Chelsa doesn't care. I *do* make cereal. To me, that's cooking, which cracks her up. And I've made her breakfast in bed a few times—eggs, toast, avocados, fruit. It really touched her that I got up early and did the one thing I hate more than anything just to see her smile. But she did not get a cook for a husband.

Now if you want someone who's going to love and adore you, someone who's going to be peaceful, respectful, caring, and kind, somebody who's going to blame you sometimes for their own upset but ultimately take responsibility and work through their own stuff, who will challenge you to work through your own stuff, help you grow, and help you love yourself more, then I'm the husband for you.

I'm also a great dad in a lot of ways, but in some ways I'm not. My daughters used to ask me to play Barbies with them, and I'd tell them, "Grandma, Mom, and you guys—you can all play Barbies, but that's not me. We can do Legos together, we can go to the park, but the Barbies thing, I'm not the dad for that."

Then I had an epiphany: I was expecting my kids to connect with me the way I want to be connected with. The next time Zoey asked me to play Barbies, I said, "All right. I don't know what to do. How do we play Barbies?" She started handing me dolls and telling me to change their outfits. I made one of my Barbies fly—Superhero Barbie. Now all my daughters make their Barbies fly.

I'm not the perfect husband, I'm not the perfect dad, but I'm aiming to get better all the time—and that's all we can do. We all have our strengths; we all have our weaknesses. We're never going to be perfect, we'll never be all things to all people, so stop trying. Find your strengths and own them.

It's worthwhile sometimes to strengthen areas where you're weak, for sure, but it's way more valuable to strengthen your strengths and own where you're great and appreciate that. Maybe one day, I'll start cooking, but if I don't, I'm going to love myself anyway. Maybe one day, I'll fix something around the house, but until then, I'm going to love myself anyway. And you can too for whatever your not-so-great areas are.

There is no such thing as perfect. Wait. That's not true. What's perfect right now is the person standing in your shoes and wearing your clothes, the person whose heart is beating, who's breathing. As you are right now, not when you finally make more money. Not when you finally buy a new outfit, get a new hairstyle, or lose weight, find love, get your kids to listen to you, or get your parents to listen to you—you right now. This is the law of perfect imperfection. It's true that you'll always be imperfect; you're human. And you will always be perfect. Not one day, when you finally heal all your stuff, but today, and every day from now on. You are amazing.

CHAPTER 10

WE HAVE ALL THE TIME IN THE WORLD

Time is the canvas on which your entire life is painted. Time is even more valuable than money. If you spend money you can make it back, but you can never get your time back. And that stresses us out. Most people don't have enough time. They feel worried, hurried, and overwhelmed—they're constantly fighting for a little bit of extra time. But when they find a bit of free time, they don't know what to do with it, and they look for ways to entertain themselves to fill the void. It's a weird dichotomy.

By now you've probably taken the Time Abundance Assessment in Chapter 2, so you'll have an idea about areas you might want to work on. In this chapter, you'll find strategies and mind-sets from my Free Your Time, Free Your Life program to help you paint an absolute masterpiece on the canvas of your life, which is your time.

How you spend your time is how you spend your life. If you want to increase the quality of your life, you need to increase the quality of how you spend your time. There are two pieces to doing that. First, you want to make sure you're doing more and more of the things you enjoy. Set yourself up so you're doing mostly things you absolutely love. Do work you love, spend your time with people you love, and do things you really enjoy.

The second piece is *how* you're doing your activities. Let's say you have a job you love. Even though you're doing work you enjoy, you might still find yourself stressed about time: *There's not enough time to get this done. I need to hurry. The boss is going to kill me if this is late.* If you're feeling that way, it greatly diminishes the quality of your time. Maybe you're at home with your family, which is one of your favorite ways to spend time, but you're stressed about work; you can't stop thinking about it. Or maybe you're at work, and your mind is on your family, and you're feeling guilty about not spending enough time at home. Either way, you're stressed about time. You're not present to the time you're spending doing what you love.

The idea is to control your time so you're doing what you want to do when you want to do it. And to be present, be in the moment. That way, while you're doing whatever activities you're doing, you're enjoying them. Of course, you can't *always* do the things you love. I have my own business, and I've set up everything so that 90 percent of the time I'm doing what I absolutely love. But now and then, I have to do something I don't. We all do. Still, you don't have to be miserable. When you're engaged in an activity you don't love, you still have the option to change how you feel about that activity, to be present, so you enjoy whatever you're doing.

One of the reasons we become overwhelmed is that we have so much to do. In our personal lives and at work, we have so many demands on our time that we start believing the lie that there's not enough time, and we start using this belief to defend ourselves from other obligations. It's time to let that go.

KEYS TO TIME ABUNDANCE

Here are four specific keys to helping you experience more time abundance in your life, starting right now.

I. Free your mind of time scarcity.

What I invite you to do is, instead of thinking you don't have enough time, start thinking you have an abundance of time. Stop saying things to yourself like, *I don't have enough time. There's so much to do and so little time. There aren't enough hours in the day.* Let's get rid of that. Those kinds of thoughts create stress. When you're stressed, you aren't enjoying your life, and you're probably not doing your best work. Plus, the more your mind is filled with time scarcity, the more you create a lack of time. It becomes a self-fulfilling prophesy.

Instead, say things to yourself like, *I have so much time and so little to do.* Or, *I have all the time in the world,* which is one of the most abundant statements about time. You'll be amazed by how it changes your perspective. Notice what it feels like to even imagine having "so little to do and so much time." It's relieving. It's expansive. It might even be a little boring. That's okay. It's a step in the right direction.

Another approach that can significantly reduce the feeling of being overwhelmed is to remember that even though we think we have so many things we need to do, there's only *one*, the one thing you're doing right now. It's all you can do. Let that sink in a bit. No matter how many things are on your plate or on your to-do list, the one thing you're doing right now is the only thing you *can* do. Be in that moment. People do their best work when they feel centered, focused, guided, and connected to Source. So why not start creating more space in your life so you can be present, in the flow, and make a bigger impact with everything you do?

2. Develop patient timelines.

Another time abundance strategy is to develop "patient timelines." Give yourself more time to complete projects than you think you need. Most tasks tend to take a little bit longer, and sometimes much longer, than we anticipate, so why not give yourself a buffer zone? Let's say that on Wednesday, your boss asks you to submit a report on Friday. If you think you can get it done by Thursday, then a Friday deadline is great. You have built-in buffer time. But if you think Friday is going to be cutting it close, you might check at that moment to see if a buffer is possible. Ask your boss, "Is there any chance we could push that due date out?" Or, "What's the situation if I get this to you by Tuesday?" Maybe you can still get it to him on Friday, or even sooner, but just see if you can push the envelope a bit.

You also want to balance priorities. If your boss, or anyone, is putting too many demands on your time, you need to say, "If I'm doing that, then there's a good chance I can't finish this. Which of these is the highest priority? Which one needs to be done sooner?" Sometimes both demands are urgent, or there are too many to keep up with. In that case, if you need help, then see if you can get it. You don't need to be in a place of crazy, pressure cooker, insane stress. Unless, for you, having a lot to do is more fun. If you enjoy your job, and you love being super busy, then great. Bring it on.

Develop patient timelines in your personal life too. If you're going to do a project around the house, think about how long it will take you to do it, and then build in buffer time. If you've ever hired a construction company to do any work for you, you know everything's going to take longer than they tell you it is. If their estimate is two weeks, it could easily take two months or longer. Contractors are notorious for underestimating how long things will take. I always assume that things are going to take a little bit longer, maybe a lot longer, than I think, and allow for the extra time. Once you set patient timelines and buffer time, you can always get things done quickly and move on to the next project, but you won't be stressed and overwhelmed in the process.

3. Love everything you do.

If you focus on doing what you love—work, projects, activities, whatever it is—you aren't going to be in a rush to get through it, because you're enjoying it. If you aren't loving a certain aspect of something you're doing, let's say it's an aspect of your job, maybe you're not good at it. We tend to enjoy things we're good at. But a lot of times, we focus on what we aren't, on strengthening our weaknesses instead of strengthening our strengths. Focus on strengthening your strengths. Do what you're good at. Do what you love. If you don't like doing something, and you're not good at it, find someone who is. Maybe you could outsource that work. Bottom line: find some other way to get it done.

Years ago, I was really bottlenecked by feeling I had to do everything in my business myself, because there were certain jobs I had to do to grow my business that I hated doing. I felt frustrated that I had to force myself to do them. Finally, I surrendered the self-loathing and the need to do everything myself. After that, I started slowly building a team of people who were better at those tasks I hated. People who loved those jobs. I started focusing on the jobs I loved to do, and my business grew much faster.

I also redistributed tasks in my personal life. In the early years of our marriage, my wife and I fought over whose turn it was to do the dishes or the laundry. We both hated those jobs. The laundry and dishes would pile up, and the piles made us grumpy. Then we surrendered to the fact that we both hated those jobs. Rather than trying to "outsmart" the other into doing what we both hated, we found a way to hire someone to do the washing for us. This was before either of us was all that financially successful, so it took some creative thinking. We moved into a less expensive apartment for a little while. What we saved in rent, we spent on extra help. We made it a priority not to fight and not to waste our energy doing what we hated. We forgave ourselves and each other for not being good at those jobs. My wife openly admits I didn't marry the kind of girl who finds pleasure in cooking and doing laundry. But that's okay, because she offers me so much more. By hiring someone to do laundry and dishes, and by not fighting about those jobs, we saved time so we could go on more dates. And we eliminated stress and friction in our relationship. We created more time and more love, which strengthened our marriage.

One of the business concepts I teach is called "cake and cringe." The things you love to do? That's your cake—you'd eat it up for breakfast every day. Then there are the things that make you cringe when you think about them. Orient your life so that you're doing more of the things you enjoy (your cake) and less of the things you don't (your cringe). Some people like working on cars. If that's you, change your own oil, and give your car a tune-up. If that's not fun for you, have someone else do it. Some people love to cook. If that's you, keep on cooking. But if you dread it, there are a lot of other options. You could hire a personal chef (which is probably the most expensive option), or you could go out to eat more often, or you could order from food prep companies that deliver ready to cook meals, or you could buy frozen foods and microwave them, or become friends with a lot of people that like to cook.

I have over 50 people that work for me in various capacities. I want them working on the things they're really good at and that they enjoy the most. I want them working in their "cake zone" because that means they'll love their job, which reduces turnover. And if everyone is working on their cake, then they're doing their best work. I don't want people on my team plodding through their work, doing stuff they aren't that great at and just trying to get through their day. The more my team is working in their cake, the better it is for them and for my business. If you work at a company that has halfway decent leadership, they'll want the same thing. And they'll be open to you rearranging your job so you're working mostly in your cake zone.

Imagine enjoying your business. Your job. Your marriage. Imagine slowly ridding yourself of the things you dread and injecting more joy and love. How much more pleasurable would your life become? And if you can't rid yourself of jobs that make you cringe, that's okay. You can still find a way to love the tasks you just can't get rid of. Do it with friends, while listening to music, or make a game out of it. You can also look for deeper meaning in doing that task. You can become present while you're doing it. Think of that task as a practice in mindfulness, a meditation. In that way, you can love everything you do.

4. Upgrade your energy sources.

People don't always like to have time on their hands. When there's little stress, they get bored, and fill up the hours with meaningless tasks or watching TV, which can drain energy. Many enjoy the stress of being busy—the chemical rush that comes from juggling too many projects or waiting until the last minute—to feel motivated and focused. But when creating time abundance, we want to get rid of those negative stressors and tap into cleaner, purer forms of energy, where we're coming from a place of peace.

To get to that place, you want to avoid negative sources of energy. Some people get energy by arguing, creating drama, by putting themselves in situations where they're constantly needed, using drugs like caffeine, or eating sugar. These are sources of energy that come at a high cost. They don't burn clean. Instead, upgrade your energy with high-quality food and water, exercising, and a great night's sleep, enabling you to be inspired, feel creative, get present, and be guided. Being guided is the ultimate energy source.

Just look at children. They spend their days creating and filling their lives with joy. They're never bored, never out of energy. My two-year-old daughter, Lily, wakes up at 6:00 A.M., bouncing up and down in her little crib, laughing and calling, "Daddy, Daddy, Daddy," while she waits for me to come get her. She then spends her entire day in a state of bubbling enthusiasm, until she fights me tooth and nail at her 7:40 P.M. bedtime, begging to stay up. Once, when my eldest daughter, Nala, was four, I asked her why she never wanted to go to sleep. She replied simply, "I like my days. I never want them to end." Wow. Something so simple but so powerful. When did we forget to "like our days"? Probably the day we bought into the story that adults must fit into pre-defined categories and do a bunch of stuff they hate in order to be productive and accepted members of society, aka that we must join the "real world."

Dirty Energy
People draw on all kinds of negative energy sources, largely, I believe, because they're not doing what brings them joy, and they need a way to fuel themselves. The energy from adrenaline can make us feel alive: *Oh, I'm in the moment. I'm in the zone.* And even though it's not necessarily the best zone, it is a zone—we're focused. But it's not a super-pure zone, because there's a lot of stress and worry in that zone.

Like adrenaline, fear can be a big driver. Many times, when I'm coaching people, they don't want to get rid of their fears, because they're afraid that, without them, they'll lose the motivation to keep working on their business or to put in as many hours. And with these people, I don't necessarily argue and tell them they need to get rid of that fear. It's their agenda, and I let them play the game they want to play; but, ideally, fear is not a great energy source. It can motivate us, there's no doubt about it, but it may not be motivating us in the best ways possible.

Then there are those who pull energy from others. In *The Celestine Prophecy,* James Redfield writes of four ways people try to steal energy in a relationship. He calls them "control dramas." The intimidators steal energy from others by threat, which makes people feel weaker and the intimidator stronger. Interrogators steal energy by judging and questioning. They grill others to prove them wrong. Aloof people act reserved or withdraw—an internal *I'm too good for you, and I don't need your love anyway*—so others have to work hard (give energy) to get their attention. And then there are those who work the "poor me" strategy, making others feel guilty and responsible for them: *I'm so troubled. I'm not that strong, and you should send me energy, because of all the stuff I've gone through.*

These are dirty forms of energy. If you think of the sources of energy we use to power our planet, these negative energies would be similar to coal or oil, sources that pollute, rather than to solar or wind energy, which are very clean. If we're relying on some of these dirtier forms of energy, it will impact the enjoyment we feel with anything we do. It affects how powerful we are in any given moment, and how effective we are in whatever we're doing. If we're using adrenaline to fuel ourselves, then that has some effectiveness, but it's not as sustainable. I'm not against any of these forms of energy. Sometimes you just need to use what you've got.

Time Warps

Often, when people are always busy and extremely driven, there's something emotional they're trying to avoid, an unresolved issue or feeling they don't want to face. One of my clients used to say "yes" to everything. He'd end up doing things and going places he didn't want because he was afraid he'd miss out on something. We've got to notice what's really going on under our busyness. Fear of missing out, fear of boredom, fear of letting people down—those are just some of the unconscious drivers of busyness. Put "do nothing time" on your calendar. Not "watch TV time" but "do nothing time." Whether you set aside 10 minutes or two hours, it doesn't matter. Go to the park and just sit. Devote time to just doing nothing. Just be there.

I think one of the reasons people have such a hard time with boredom is that when they're in that place, they're left with just themselves and their feelings, and they have a hard time fully feeling and being present. In my Free Your Time, Free Your Life program, I ask participants to set the intention of being bored as much as they can for a month. I urge you to do the same. Why? If you can make your life more boring, that's a good thing for a little while. Also, slowing down how we do things and how we live our lives actually speeds up the time it takes to get the results we want.

Time is very warpable. I once listened to an interview with NFL quarterback Steve Young who said that, in his first season, he couldn't believe how much faster everything moved in the NFL versus college football. As you get older, he said, and more experienced, the game starts to slow down, and time stretches out a bit more. He said that, for an NFL quarterback, there's a sweet spot, a window where you're still strong, athletic, and powerful, but time has slowed down enough that you feel like you can make crisper decisions. You're a much, much better quarterback.

I think one of the reasons the game might feel so much faster in the beginning is that when players first get to professional football, they've got so much adrenaline going. Eventually, they become more patient, relaxed, and able to anticipate what's going to happen next, so there's not so much excitement and adrenaline going on. It's still fun, but there's a lot more of the peaceful presence that many great quarterbacks experience.

Renewable Energy Sources

Getting to that place where time warps, where your energy comes from a place of peace and heightened intuition, you'll not only need to draw on positive energy sources, you'll also need to know how you recharge. We've all heard the terms "introvert" and "extrovert." Many people believe an extrovert is someone who's outgoing and social, and an introvert is someone who's antisocial and shy. But the terms refer to the way you renew your energy. Extroverts feel energized by crowds and love being around people. Although I used to be shy when I was a kid, I'm very social and outgoing now, but I don't get energy from being in a crowd. Many times, crowds will drain my energy. If my energy is low, I usually want to go home or be by myself to refuel. Notice where you get energy around people. Do you get more energy in crowds, or do you get more energy being alone? Notice that and honor that for yourself.

You also want to pay attention to emotions that drain you, and those that give you clean energy. Negative emotions such as fear, obligation, worry, anger, guilt, and shame drain your energy. The more you resolve these draining emotions, the cleaner, lighter, and brighter your energy will be. You'll have more power and you'll experience emotions that raise your energy—love, joy, passion, devotion, gratitude, inspiration, and peace.

Start thinking about what you can build into your environment or your life that will inspire you and allow you feel to more gratitude, more peace, more joy. What can you do to activate these purer, higher-level emotions? Who can you surround yourself with? What can you notice right now about your friends and co-workers, or even your family, that inspires you?

EIGHT DAYS A WEEK

You can make these changes. You can increase your joy, the quality of your time abundance—time you fill with doing what you love, surrounded by people who uplift you. Remember, you are infinitely powerful. What would you do if you had all the time in the world? What would you do if you had total time freedom to do whatever you want to do with whomever you want to do it, wherever you want to do it? Where would you go? What would you do? Who would you hang out with? What would you do if you could add an extra day to your week, so instead of having seven days a week you'd have eight? Would you catch up on all the things you need to catch up on? Would you sleep in? Would you take a day trip, just do something fun?

Whatever most people would do with that day, it would change their lives for a little while, then they'd get so used to having that extra day it would become like all the other days of the week, and they'd feel just as overwhelmed as they always have. Why is that? Why is it that we have total control of all seven days of the week, that we can decide how much time we want to spend doing the things we want to do, yet we don't?

Sure, you might have a regular job working a certain number of hours a week, but you have all the time in the morning before work. In the evening. On weekends, holidays, and "well days" (when you can take off from work just because you're happy, feeling good, and want to take time off). We've got time, yet often, most of us fill that time with just getting things done. If we have something exciting going on in our lives, we're more likely to wrap our time around it, instead of just surfing the web or watching TV and letting our free time pass us by.

I'll leave you with these questions: What would you really like to do during those free hours? What excites you? And what would it take to get you to do more of that all the time?

CHAPTER 11

SUCCESS IS INEVITABLE

Anything you want, you can have. You just have to (1) decide what you want, and (2) decide to have it, be it, or do it. Many years ago, I heard that becoming a millionaire wasn't a goal, it was a decision. If you want to be a millionaire, don't *hope* to be a millionaire, *decide* to be a millionaire. There's a huge difference, right?

When I started my coaching business, I didn't think it was possible for me to make big money as a personal-success coach. In fact, I wasn't even thinking about the money. I just thought that if I could make as much as I'd made in my last regular job ($35,000 a year), I'd be living the dream. Do what I love most for a living and still pay my bills? Sign me up. I felt excited and inspired, and those emotions fueled my motivation.

I eventually reached the $35,000 mark, with a lot of pain, sweat, and tears. Then I heard about coaches making six figures, and I thought, *Oh, man, make $100,000 a year? I want to do that.* So I set that as my goal, which felt like . . . *Whoa.* I couldn't even imagine it. My goal felt impossible.

The way $1 million might feel to some. But I set it. And I reached it. It took me another three years, but I did it. Then I set another goal. And another. And eventually I grew my business into a multi-million-dollar global enterprise.

ONE STEP AT A TIME

Here's a key to setting goals: break them down into milestones that challenge you without seeming unreachable. This way you don't get discouraged and you stay motivated. Success follows a continuum. Each step builds on the one before. If you want to lose 35 pounds, your first milestone should be to lose 1 pound. If you want to make a million dollars, your first milestone is dollar one. The milestones might look like this: $1, $1,000, $5,000, $10,000 per month; $250,000 per year; $500,000 per year; $750,000 per year; $1 million per year.

In our society, we tend to want everything instantly. We don't like to wait. But we have to remember that all great things come from humble beginnings. Starbucks didn't start with 22,000 stores. They started with one. Famous basketball legend Michael Jordan took his very first shot as a little kid, and he probably missed. And he definitely wasn't slamming down dunks from the free-throw line at that age. If you want success, you're going to take it one step at a time.

I believe success is inevitable if you're willing to do the work in the world, if you're willing to do the work on yourself, and if you never give up. It's that last one that's the tricky one—never giving up. I wanted to give up so many times in the early years of my business. But I didn't, and now I'm a multimillionaire. I have fancy cars, nice clothes, and multiple million-dollar estates. And even more rewarding, I have an incredible family I love and adore, and great friendships. It wasn't easy. I had to learn a lot and grow a lot to get here. It took time. Much of what I learned is in this book. This book is the shortcut to having what you want. You can't skip the work, but you can speed things up tremendously. And much of what we really want is available instantly simply by practicing more gratitude.

Many people have a lot of uncertainty about being able to get what they want: *What if it doesn't work? What if I fail? What if I get rejected? What if I get fired? Can I really make it happen?* The answer is YES you can. You can have whatever you want. And you absolutely *will* have it, if you're willing to take these steps:

1. Take action to make it happen, and keep taking action until you get what you want. The 5-Step Rapid Success System can be a huge help with this step.

2. Work on yourself to release the fears, doubts, and limiting beliefs that might hold be holding you back.

- Take the Abundance Assessments in Chapter 2 or online at www.Abundance Score.com, where you'll also get exclusive access to a special Infinite Abundance training video.

- Use the Peace Process. You can also visit www.PeaceProcessNow.com to watch examples of me taking people through the Peace Process, and to download a Peace Process guided meditation, where I'll take you through the Peace Process.

- Go to www.InstantMiracleExperience. com to witness healings on people who may have challenges similar to yours, and to experience the healing as well.

Don't give up. Your success is inevitable. It's just a matter of time. Time is the only unknown. How fast will it happen? When you operate from the world of "water" (remember rock, taffy, water?), and let yourself be guided—by God, your intuition, your higher self, whatever you connect with that guides you—it usually happens a lot faster.

FAILURE IS INEVITABLE

On the other hand, the more you go after your dreams, the more you will fail because failure is also inevitable. In fact, that's the *only* way to achieve success. You have to go through the failures to achieve great success. In fact, failures are the bricks that pave the way to success. It's much better to live a life chasing your dreams and scraping your knees along the way, than to live a safe life with few failures but never tasting victory or success. As author John A. Shedd wrote, "A ship in harbor is safe—but that is not what ships are built for."

**In fact, failures are the bricks
that pave the way to success.**

The biggest successes are often the people who are willing to take risks and fail the most. J. K. Rowling, the wildly successful billionaire author of the Harry Potter series, originally failed on an epic scale. When she spoke at the commencement ceremony for the Harvard University class of 2008, she talked about her own failures, just seven years out of college. Her marriage had gone bust. She was a single mom. She had no job. She was one step from being homeless. All her fears had been realized. "By every usual standard," she said, "I was the biggest failure I knew. I had no idea then how far the tunnel extended, and for a long time, any light at the end of it was a hope, rather than a reality."

To J. K. Rowling, the benefit of failing so monumentally was "a stripping away of the inessential." She was who she was. No pretenses. She could do what mattered to her, and that was to write her books. "So rock bottom," she said, "became the solid foundation on which I rebuilt my life." Wow. She went on to say that failure inevitably happens, that "it is impossible to live without failing at something, unless you live so cautiously that you might as well not have lived at all, in which case you fail by default." The knowledge that you have emerged wiser and stronger from setbacks means that you're ever-after secure in your ability to survive. You will never truly know yourself or the strength of your relationships until both have been tested by adversity.

There's no way to succeed without failing. The only way to make millions is to "mistake your way to millions." You have to put yourself out there. You have to keep going for it no matter how crazy things get. In baseball, the hitters who are successful only one-third of the time are considered superstars. That's a two-thirds fail rate. Two-thirds. And they keep stepping up to the plate. They keep swinging. When I started my business as a success coach, I was scared to death of failing. I toiled away in self-doubt and agony: *Who am I to be a coach? I'm only 24. What the heck do I know? Is anybody going to hire me?* I had to do what seemed like a million one-off sessions where I charged nothing or very little. I had no clients with long-term commitments. Then a few people paid, I got a taste of what was possible, and that taste kept me going. But it was tough.

One day, after about two years of struggling, I was taking out the garbage, and I thought, *Man, you know, maybe it would be easier to just become a garbageman, because I wouldn't have to think so hard, and my struggles would be over. Plus, I'd get union benefits.* For a moment, it actually sounded like a great idea. Then I thought about what Kahlil Gibran wrote in *The Prophet:* "Work is love made visible. And if you can't work with love, but only with distaste, it is better that you should leave your work and sit at the gate of the temple and take alms of the people who work with joy."

I loved being a coach, and I knew being a garbageman was not work I'd love. It just seemed like an easy way out (not that being a garbage man is an easy job). The few paying clients I had, and the friends I coached for free, kept telling me I was making such a big difference in their lives, and I felt I was doing the work I should be doing. I had to do what I was born to do. There was no other way. I had to do it even if I lost my house and my car trying to make it work. I was willing to let it all go.

Something shifted inside me that day. I felt that if I failed financially, that was okay, because I was doing the work I loved, and I was helping people. Maybe I would lose my house and my car. If so, I imagined I would wander from town to town the way David Carradine did in the '70s TV show *Kung Fu*. I used to watch the reruns growing up. Maybe you remember it. Carradine plays a Buddhist monk trained in the martial art of kung fu. He wanders the Old West, taken in by strangers who want to help him out. Instead, he's often called upon to help them out by stopping the local bad guys with his kung fu.

I saw myself roaming from town to town just like the monk, Grasshopper—homeless, people taking me in, wanting to help—but I'd really help them more with my coaching. I would do "Coach Fu." At the time, I lived in Chicago. My plan was to be homeless someplace warm—heading homelessly south, coaching people as I wandered, making my way in the world. With that plan in place, I surrendered my need to show people I was rich and hugely successful, and that was a huge turning point for me.

CELEBRATE FAILURE

When Sara Blakely, the founder of the "shapewear" company Spanx, was growing up, every night at dinner her father asked her and her brother what they'd failed at that day. He celebrated their failures, because they'd put themselves out there. He even had them write down the hidden gifts in their experiences. So for her, to fail meant not to try. One time, she told him she'd failed at cheerleading tryouts, and he high-fived her.

In a July 2016 interview with *Business Insider*, Blakely said, "So many people don't take risks for fear of failure. They don't start the business, they don't go create the art they want to create, or they don't go try out to be in the play, or whatever it is, for the fear of failure. Once you redefine that for yourself and realize that the failure is just not trying, then life opens up to you in many ways."

At Spanx, Sara Blakely celebrates failure, and feels that if you can learn from it, or laugh about it, it's all worth it. She has a $23 billion business.

Most of us feel that failure is bad. Some of us probably were taught that "It's safer to just not try." Or: "Don't get your hopes up." Or worse: "Do I really have that much to offer?"

Whatever it is you want, you can have. Now maybe there are some things in which you might not succeed. Finding holes in this theory of success is inevitable. You could find something that's seemingly impossible. Say you set your sights on breathing underwater without an oxygen tank. Probably not going to happen. Then again, you could reframe that thought, because at some point, somebody wanted to breathe underwater—they had that vision—and they invented a way to do that with scuba diving equipment. That was the impossible, and then it became possible because somebody decided, "I want to figure out how to do this. I want to be able to see all the life under the water." And they did.

LAW OF ATTRACTION

In 2002, I had the good fortune of going to an Abraham-Hicks event. Jerry and Esther Hicks wrote the book *The Law of Attraction*. I got to ask questions and work with Abraham, whom Esther channels. I got to ask seven questions. It was awesome. I love what they teach about the Law of Attraction, that what we can imagine and what we emotionally feel good about, we attract into our lives.

The challenge is that most of us have mixed feelings about what we want. We want more money, but if we had that money, it might be scary: *What are people going to think of me if I'm rich? Are people going to think I'm greedy or I'm bad? Or is someone going to try to take it away? Or maybe I'll just lose it anyway.* Whatever messed-up programming we have about money, we might want it, but we probably also have some baggage around it. Or maybe we really want to be in a relationship, but when we think about finding love once more, it scares us, because we don't want our heart broken again. When we want something, and we're also afraid of it, we pull it partway toward us, but keep it at arm's length.

If we're Law-of-Attracting it, and focusing on "I want more money in my life," but we have the shadow side of the things we want, then we'll probably end up (1) not manifesting it, (2) manifesting it really slowly, (3) manifesting it and getting rid of it quickly, or (4) getting some watered-down version of it, where we get some of what we want but not enough to frighten us; so, ultimately, it's not what we really want. Those blocking fears, limiting beliefs, and rigid (rock) ways of thinking put a kink in our firehose of abundance.

By using the tools in this book, you'll release these kinks and get to a place of peace, so you can receive more of the good things you want in life. So many amazing things happen when you're at peace, when you let go of the "charge" or "trigger" that's keeping the thing you want from happening, and when you have the courage to step up despite any fears. I know there are people who really are more strategic and scientific and might think that that kind of Law of Attraction just isn't true. And that's okay.

I'm not trying to convince you of anything. I'm not here to convince you that Instant Miracle is real. You can see for yourself. The proof is in the pudding. But I know, for me, when I let go of my blocks, my fears, my challenges—especially when I let go of my fear of getting the things that I want—suddenly, magical things happen. You get introduced to the right person. A great opportunity arises. Years ago, I had the thought that I should be the new leader of the personal-coaching industry. I was still very young and pretty much an unknown in the field. I feared what people would think of me if I told anyone. But I did the Peace Process on my fears of being judged, and a few days later, totally out of the blue, I got a call from someone at *Forbes* magazine wanting to interview me for an article on coaching. My first big break!

MIRACLES WILL SHOW UP

As I've said, the only mystery to manifesting is time. The only mystery to success is time—how long is it going to take for you to be successful? No one knows. Quitting is the only surefire way to squelch your success. You don't know if you're going to manifest what you want in one week, one month, one year, or longer, but when you work through this stuff, well, I've been blown away by how fast opportunities can show up.

One of my friends is a very well-known CEO of a successful company. I wanted him to promote a program for me. He had said he was going to, but hadn't yet, and the window for my promotion was closing. I started feeling frustrated and mad at him. But I realized that, deep down, my real fears were that I wasn't important to him and that my promotion wasn't going to do well without his support. He's a great person, a good friend, and he'd done so much for me before. Instead of being bitter about what I wasn't getting, I knew I needed to be in a place of gratitude for that friendship. So I Peace-Processed and Instant-Miracled my fears and frustrations and let them go. Not 10 minutes later, I checked my inbox, and I had an e-mail from him: "Hey. I have this promotional e-mail going out for you right now. Sorry I wasn't able to jump in sooner." It's amazing how fast miracles can show up when you let go of your stuff.

A client of mine had a fear of public speaking. We Peace-Processed and Instant-Miracled it, and she let that go. Almost immediately, out of nowhere, people started asking her to speak for different conferences. She had five speaking gigs within two weeks after letting go of that fear. Miracles will happen.

"The journey of a thousand miles starts with a single step," Lao-tzu said. This is very true. But if you don't keep walking, you'll never reach your destination.

Whatever your goals and dreams are, stick with them. Take the first step and keep on walking. You'll get there. Your success is inevitable.

CHAPTER 12

YOU ARE INFINITELY POWERFUL

You are infinitely powerful, infinitely creative, and infinitely resourceful.

Before we're born, we're all swimming around as part of the infinite, all-powerful creator of everything. Completely connected with God, all our needs are met. We want for nothing. We feel infinite love and abundance. God takes tiny drops of Its infinite power, which is our spirit, and puts us into the physical world as helpless little babies.

We are infinitely powerful, infinitely creative, and infinitely resourceful. But in our new physical form, we start out as completely helpless babies who can't scratch an itch, can't walk, can't talk, can't help around the house, can't make any money, and can't pay any bills. All we can do is eat, poo, and cry. And we do a lot of all three for quite a while. As we grow, we can do much more, but we're still so much less powerful than kids who are older than we are, stronger than we are, or smarter than we are. And adults are powerful giants compared to us.

We feel weak, small, and not all that great or powerful compared to so many people around us. We grow up believing we aren't smart enough, strong enough, pretty enough, or good enough. And we get indoctrinated into the world of scarcity. There isn't enough time. There isn't enough money. Love can be withdrawn at any moment. We develop limiting beliefs about ourselves. We restrict ourselves from being all we could be. We forget our infinite selves.

When I was 12, I watched a show about how elephants are trained. When an elephant is a baby, the trainers put a chain around its leg to keep it from running away. As the elephant grows bigger, the trainers don't even need a chain; they just use a light rope. Even though the elephant is bigger and stronger and can easily break free from the rope, it's learned that it couldn't get away from the chain, so it's stopped trying. It doesn't even realize the chain isn't there anymore. It just "knows" it's stuck. We humans are like that. When we're little, we learn we can't do things, and then we just think that's the way it is. When I was six years old, I "learned" I wasn't good at sports. My two older brothers were much better than I was. And my neighbor was *waaay* better.

When I was in fifth grade, we discovered I needed glasses. I wore my new glasses to Little League practice, stepped up to the plate to bat, and *actually hit the ball!* Until that moment, I thought sports was just something some people were good at and some people weren't. I assumed I was one of the ones who weren't. End of story. I didn't realize that good eyesight was an important factor, or that lots of practice could help me become very good. I'd also started school at four instead of five, so I was smaller than the other kids, which didn't help.

Sure, some kids have more natural talent than others, but age difference, practice, and good vision matter too. Now I realize that if I'd shown a genuine interest in sports, had support and instruction, practiced, and had my vision corrected sooner, I could have been a decent athlete. Maybe even a really good one. But by the time I got my glasses, it was too late. I'd already decided, *I'm not good at sports*, and mostly avoided sports for fear of embarrassment for the rest of my school years. I was just like the elephant with a thin rope chaining me into believing I could never be good at sports.

I forgot my infinite self. I forgot that, deep down, we have that infinite power. Inside each of us is the same power that dreamed up skyscrapers, invented airplanes, put people into outer space, created amazing works of art, saved millions of lives, and inspired entire generations of people.

MAKING WAY FOR MAGIC

The fact that any of us can do amazing things is proof that we all can. We just need to find our strengths and passions, develop our talents, let go of our doubts and fears, and take bold, consistent action to manifest all that we want in life. We all push away what we want most in life. We all have blocks to getting what we want. We can get past them. If you let yourself relax and surrender to the amazing power that's within us all, you'll experience more and more magic and miracles coming into your life. The abundance techniques in this book can help change and heal so many blocks to that magic.

At my seminars, I often ask people to list their accomplishments—big, small, it doesn't matter—just write down whatever they can remember. Whatever comes to mind. When they finish their lists, most of them find they have far more accomplishments than they had realized or given themselves credit for. Then I have them look at what helped them achieve those successes—what inside them allowed for that magic to come in. I ask them to tap into that power. When they do, they find strengths they had no idea they possessed, strengths they can draw on to create amazing lives.

But sometimes we can be in such a bad space that it's hard to find the great things about ourselves and the miracles in our lives, to realize how powerful we are. Doing the work to get out of that space can be extremely painful, but in the end, it can be more painful not to do it. And when we do the work, we make way for miracles. I've sure been in that space, many times. In the early days of my business, I relocated from Chicago to San Diego. I wasn't making much money yet, and

I'd had to leave behind the client list and network I'd developed. When I got to San Diego, right off the bat, I started going to lots of networking mixers. Finally, I decided to host my own. I did everything I could to get people to come to the mixer, to see the value in attending. I *really* wanted more people to be there. And I was so worried they wouldn't come. I was coming from a needy, desperate space.

The night before the mixer, only 15 people had confirmed. Only 15. I was in agony about it. It would have been far better if no one had confirmed than just the few who did. If no one had registered, I could have canceled the event. Fifteen was a very small group, but a group nonetheless. And who knew how many would actually show up—12, 10, 8? I was so worried, my mind wouldn't shut down: *If only a few people show up, it's gonna look really bad. It's not much of a networking event if there aren't many people there to network with. The event will be a failure. I'll be a failure. I'm new in town, and people will think I'm a loser. People are going to be unhappy that they wasted their time.*

I tried everything I could think of to distract myself. I hopped in the hot tub, drank a margarita—anything to avoid the feelings of anxiety and dread. But at that point, there was nothing else I could do to convince people to come, so I went to bed, where I tossed and turned, mind racing, unable to sleep until I decided I had to surrender to what I was feeling. At that time, I was just discovering and developing the Peace Process, so I Peace-Processed myself. I tuned in, focused on where my feelings were most intense, and started surrendering to the feeling, letting it go, letting it go.

I realized that my biggest fear about the mixer had nothing to do with business and everything to do with the anxiety and fear I felt when I was a kid, constantly wondering, *Am I one of the cool kids? Am I popular? Am I wanted? Am I accepted?* The situation of the head count at my mixer did not match the intensity of emotion I was feeling—like I was going to die. It just didn't match up mathematically and logically. But our emotions aren't logical. That intense anxiety is our caveman brain talking, the reptilian part of our brain that lives in fight-or-flight survival mode. My wondering if I was going to fit in and be accepted goes back to the whole fitting-in thing from our caveman days, when being a part of a tribe meant survival, and being out of the tribe meant almost certain death.

When we can release those fears, we find that there's so much going on beneath those fears, so much that goes deeper. What's so amazing is that when we heal one fear, we can heal a thousand different pieces of our psyche and our identity; all kinds of issues about work, dating and relationships, and our health. Each fear we surrender to heals so much of ourselves.

That night, I Peace-Processed all my fears and anxiety until I felt totally neutral about the number of people attending. The next morning, I went to my mixer. And instead of 15 people or fewer showing up,

18 people came. A few people had asked a friend at the last minute. It ended up being a great event. People really enjoyed meeting each other, but they also were happy to meet me. They were happy with what I taught. And I ended up getting a few clients from that event. My Peace-Processing cleared layers of fear *and* made way for miracles—a solid showing at my mixer, people who loved my work, and new clients so I could continue to build my business in this new town.

PLAYING TO YOUR STRENGTHS

Playing to our strengths is crucial. It's what brings us joy, taps into what we're here to do. As I've said, most people focus on strengthening their weaknesses. When I was a kid, all I wanted to do was work at a comic-book store. I finally got a job working at one, and I loved it. It was my dream job. My boss was super happy with how I handled customers. That was my strength—helping people. I was also responsible for cashing out at the end of the day, which was one of my weaknesses: simple math. At the end of the day, I had to count the money in the till—tally the credit-card receipts, count the cash, and write down the total amount of pennies, nickels, dimes, quarters, dollar bills—all of it. I'd subtract the amount we always kept in the drawer, and lock the earnings in the safe. I used a calculator. I was so careful. One day, my boss came up to me and said, "The amount you're saying is in the drawer isn't matching what's actually there.

What's going on here? Either you're putting money in, or you're taking money out, but something's not right, and this isn't the first time you've been off."

I apologized all over the place. "Oh, man. I'll try to do my best. I'll do better." And I thought I'd have no problem. *Okay,* I thought. *I can do this. A seven-year-old could do this. I've got it.* Only I didn't have it.

A couple of weeks later, he came up to me again. "Dude, you're still not getting it right."

"All right," I said, "I can do this." But by then, it didn't seem so easy. I wasn't so sure I could get it right.

But I tried. I developed a new system. I counted the money, wrote down the amount, and then counted it again. The first total never matched the second, so I'd count it a third time. That total never matched either of the first two, so I'd go with whichever of the first two totals came closest to the third. I felt really dumb. I felt like, *Man, what's wrong with me? Why can't I get this right? How am I going to understand any other kind of stuff?* I was all stressed out, which probably made me screw up even more. I felt flat-out incompetent and ashamed. Eventually, I got fired. It was heartbreaking. And my boss was sad to let me go because he really loved how I worked with customers, but being able to calculate the drawer accurately was critical to his business.

Shortly after that, I got another job. This time I was working at UPS. My job was to sort the packages by zip codes and put them in the right bin. I was going too slow. My bosses told me to go faster. When

I went faster, I made lots of mistakes. What made matters worse was that the same day they hired me, they also hired one of the greatest package sorters in UPS history. She was crazy fast and very accurate. I knew I was failing, and there wasn't much I could do about it. That job lasted about 30 days. That was two back-to-back confidence-busting jobs early in my working career. Looking back now, it's a good thing I wasn't great at those jobs, because maybe I'd still be working at the comic-book store or UPS. But at the time it was demoralizing.

Now that I'm the boss of my own business, with more than 50 people who work for me, I don't need to do the work I'm not good at or that I don't enjoy—two things that, as I've said, pretty much go hand in hand. I can assign the task to someone who's great at it and who loves it, which is what I recommend for everyone—the cake-and-cringe principle that I mentioned in Chapter 10. In the same vein, in my company, I want to make sure people are doing what they love and working to their strengths.

Of course, not everyone owns their own business, but you can always present a case to your boss so you can do the work you're good at and that you love. And if that doesn't work, maybe you'll need to find another job. When I worked at the comic-book shop, my boss hated to let me go, because he thought I was fantastic with customers. He felt I was great in a lot of ways, but counting the drawer wasn't one of them. I wish it had been possible for someone else to count the drawer, but in that job, we had only one person working per shift, so he had to let me go.

When you screw things up, it's so easy to think, *Wow, there's something wrong with me;* to be ashamed, and to take that one problem and globalize it to your whole identity. *I can't count. I'm a loser. I'll never amount to anything. I'll never succeed. No one will ever want to date me. I might as well throw in the towel right now.* We look at how we're successful or unsuccessful in one area and extend it to our whole life. We think, *Wow, if I can't do that, maybe I can't really do much of anything.* The truth is that I suck at counting. Sometimes I can do math in my head and come up with the right number, and I feel really proud of myself. But overall, it's just not where my strength lies. But the thing is, just because I'm bad at math doesn't mean I'm bad at everything.

Everyone has strengths. A lot of people know what their strengths are. Many don't. Most of us downplay our strengths. We don't even realize they're strengths, because we just think that if something is easy for us, it's probably easy for most people. We don't even realize that maybe we actually have some genius in a certain area. But we do. When we find out we have a weakness, what do we usually try to do? We try to strengthen that weakness, when the best bet is to find your strengths and strengthen your strengths. Get better at the things you're good at. Whenever I failed, especially in the early days of my career, it was so easy to beat myself up: *I suck at counting. I can't count. How can I run a business if I can't count?* I finally got to the place of acceptance. It's not the end of the world. That's just how it is. But we all have the tendency to pile on the shame, self-judgment, embarrassment.

We are infinitely powerful. You are infinitely powerful. You are a piece of the divine plucked from the oneness of God.

DON'T JUDGE A FISH BY ITS INABILITY TO CLIMB A TREE

Einstein said, "If you judge a fish by its ability to climb a tree, it will live its whole life believing that it is stupid." I've gotten better at counting and finances over the years, but sometimes I still make mistakes. You don't want me to be your bookkeeper. I will tell you that. But that's not really the point. The point is that not being able to count is not the sum total of who I am—I have other strengths. And weaknesses.

I am one hell of a husband and one hell of a father. But I also suck as a father and a husband. There are things I'm great at when it comes to being a dad and being a husband, and there are things I'm not that great at. Some of my wife's friends' husbands are really handy. They can fix things around the house. They can put up curtain rods and fix doorknobs. But just because I'm not handy around the house, doesn't mean I'm a bad husband, or a rotten human being. Another one of my wife's friends has a husband who's practically a gourmet chef. As I've said, I hate to cook. I don't like to clean either. I guess some people might say I'm pretty lazy. Maybe so. But I am very patient, kind, levelheaded, loving, and supportive of my wife and the kids. I don't yell and scream. I look for the best in people. I'm playful and don't take myself or life too seriously (most of the time).

The bottom line is that we all have areas where we're great and areas where we're not. I think it's time to stop apologizing for the areas you're not great and just forgive yourself and surrender to that. We're not perfect. And yet, you're perfect just the way you are. You may have heard that before and thought, *Oh, yeah. We're perfect the way we are*, and yet you might think, *But I'm all messed up in these ways*. Well, I'm here to tell you it's okay. It's okay to be you, and it's a blessing to be you. The more "you" you decide to be, starting now, the better the world is going to be, because the world doesn't need more people trying to be perfect, falling short, apologizing, and trying to work at being really good in areas where they're weak.

The world needs people who are authentically themselves. The world needs to be filled with people who are being their best selves, who know their strengths, who live their strengths, and who let go where they're not strong. You are infinitely powerful, infinitely creative, and infinitely resourceful. You can have anything you want. You can be anything you want. You can do anything you want. You can live the life you want right now. The biggest thing standing in the way of all the abundance and success you want are your fears, doubts, and limiting thinking, and you can heal those. Commit to healing those blocks. Starting now.

YOU HAVE A BIG DESTINY

I want to leave you with just one final thought, which is this: You have a big destiny, much bigger than you can see, much bigger than you realize. You're here to serve, heal, love, support, uplift, and inspire others. You wouldn't be reading this book otherwise. You wouldn't be doing this inner work. You wouldn't be doing all you could to be the best you can be, to create the best life possible. Because when you create that life, it uplifts others too. Your destiny is to inspire lots of people just by who you are and who you're becoming. And with a big destiny comes a big responsibility. You can't play small. You can't hide out. I get that there are going to be days when you just want to go under the covers and not get out of bed. That's okay, that's normal, that's natural. Take a day, take two days, but then get yourself out of bed and get back out there, because people need you. You are needed.

You're on the fast track to growth. The techniques in this book are on the cutting edge of healing and personal growth. You're reading this book for a reason. Even if you don't know what that reason is. You have work to do. You can have the life you want, the relationship you want, the career you want, the success you want. You just have to stick with it. And you have to be willing to start small to get big.

Why doubt yourself? You don't have to be a big expert right off. You don't have to have all of the answers. You don't have to be a certain age. You can be really young. You can be really old. You could have zero experience and no clue. All that matters is that you want to play big and lead a bigger life. You just have to get in the game.

You don't have to have all this stuff figured out. You never will, anyway. You don't have to have all the answers, because you never will. Get comfortable with "I don't know." You don't need to know. Then the more comfortable you are with not knowing, the more you kind of just figure it out, and the answers come. Trust that the answers will come. Trust in yourself. Surrender to the process. Make room for your amazingness. Make room for miracles.

CONCLUSION

Now that you've come to the end of this book, I want you to reflect on the past few days, weeks, or however long it's taken you to read it. You might review notes you've taken about what you wanted to let go of before you started this journey, or discovered that you want to let go of as you read. I encourage you to take the Abundance Assessments again—either in the book or online (www.AbundanceScore.com)—to check your progress. Now's a great time to jot down what's changed for you, whether you feel different, and how you feel different. What's possible for you now? What's your vision for success? What do you want to achieve next from here? What are you most looking forward to? What are you most excited about now?

Wherever you are in your journey, the next level of success is at hand. Love yourself. Forgive yourself. You are amazing. You are amazing. You are amazing. There's no one on Earth better than you. No one can be a better you than you. This is your journey, your story, your life. It's to be lived by you in the greatest and best way possible.

"Whatever you can do," Goethe said, "or dream you can do, begin it. Boldness has genius, power, and magic in it." Be bold! You have a powerful spirit inside of you, and nothing can stop that spirit's expansion but you. Nothing can keep you from anything you want, except you. Everything you want in life is trying to get in: more money, health, love, time, and more abundance overall are all trying to come into your life. Happiness and success are trying to get in, just by your mere desire for them. Dream big. Commit to your success. Commit to sticking with it. And be ready to receive the miracles that await you.

You are infinitely powerful.
You are swimming in oceans of abundance.
You are loved, deeply loved.
You have all the time in the world.
Your success is inevitable.
You are the miracle.
You can have all the love, money, sex,
fame, fortune, peace, love,
and happiness you could ever want.
Go out and enjoy your life.
Live the life of your dreams.

RESOURCES

Take the Abundance Assessments online to chart your abundance levels and watch yourself get more and more abundant over time. www.AbundanceScore.com

Healing and Abundance Programs:

The Instant Miracle Abundance Program

In this online training program, you'll experience the Instant Miracle Technique that releases your blocks and opens the floodgates to massive abundance.

Enjoy:

- More money
- More love
- More health
- More time
- More freedom
- More happiness

www.InstantMiracleAbundance.com

The More Money Program: How to Get More Money, Save More Money, Spend More Money, Give More, and Live More . . . Starting Right Now

In this powerful 3-part audio program, you will:

- Turn yourself into a money-attracting magnet.

- Uncover your unconscious financial "blueprint"/money patterns, so that you can resolve them once and for all.

- Discover the underlying factors that could be keeping you weak, small, and powerless, so that you can release them and unleash the huge, strong, and powerful person you were born to be!

www.TheMoreMoneyProgram.com

Free Your Time, Free Your Life: The Time Abundance Program

Most "time management" programs don't actually get you more "free time." This program is different. It will transform your relationship with time altogether.

In this powerful 7-module program, you'll discover:

- How to free your mind of time scarcity, so "not enough time" is rarely if ever an issue for you again

- How to develop patient timelines so you have plenty of time and space to make your biggest goals become reality while you enjoy the entire process

- How to set up your life so that you LOVE everything you do (imagine that!)
- And so much more.

www.FreeYourTimeFreeYourLife.com
Attend one of my upcoming healing events:

Instant Miracle Experience (IMX)

Here's a sneak-peek into some of the breakthroughs you'll experience at this powerful event . . .

- *The Instant Success Formula:* Uncover what causes your inner blocks and how to free yourself from them
- *Miraculous Health:* Heal the inner blocks that have been causing serious health changes
- *Finally in Love Forever:* Remove fear of rejection so you can attract the relationship of your dreams and be in love forever
- *More Money Miracles:* Understand the "secret psychology" behind money and how to get a lot more of it
- *The Time Freedom Formula:* Discover the only four time-management techniques that actually work and why traditional time-management techniques do not "give you more time"
- *The Miracle of Happiness:* Learn how to be happy while you attract the people, career, health, money and things that you really want

Find out more and get your ticket to the next IMX event here . . .

www.InstantMiracleExperience.com

Instant Miracle Mastery

At this powerful, four-day live certification event, you will master . . .

- The Instant Miracle Technique
- The Peace Process
- Muscle Testing
- Energy Healing

You'll be certified as an Instant Miracle Master!

Plus you'll also get tons of healing for yourself the entire time.

To learn more and get registered for the next Instant Miracle Mastery event, go to www.InstantMiracleM-astery.com

Start and Grow Your Own Coaching or Healing Business with these great resources . . .

Books:

How to Quickly Get Started as a Personal Coach: Get Paid Big Money to Change People's Lives

Get Clients Today: 3 Simple Steps to All the Clients You Want

Change the World: And Make Big Money Teaching, Training, and Serving Humanity

Online Training Programs:
The Professional Coaching Quick Start Kit: Get Started Quickly as a Professional Coach
In this training, you'll discover . . .

- How to get started in coaching as a new career or business

- How to get paid to help people make changes

- Why people hire a coach and how much coaches make

- Bonus: Includes my #1 best-selling book *How to Quickly Get Started as a Personal Coach: Get Paid Big Money to Change People's Lives*

- Plus, much, much more

To learn more and register for the Coaching Quick Start Kit, go to . . .
www.CoachingQuickStartKit.com

Free Sessions That Sell: The Client Sign-Up System

- Discover how to get lots of high-paying coaching, consulting, or healing clients
- Create a relentless demand and a waiting list of clients wanting to work with you
- Know exactly what to say and do to get clients to hire you, right on the spot

To learn more and to join, go to . . .
www.FreeSessionsThatSell.com

ACKNOWLEDGMENTS

My life is one big case of "standing on the shoulders of giants." I'm a voracious learner—especially when it comes to personal growth. I want to thank Dan Millman, Eckhart Tolle, Thomas Leonard, Tony Robbins, Don Miguel Ruiz, Raphael Cushnir, Tom Stone, Neale Donald Walsch, Byron Katie, Paulo Coelho, James Redfield, and many others whose work has inspired me, opened my mind, and opened my heart.

I also want to thank Reid Tracy for encouraging me to write this book, Kelly Malone for helping me with editing, and my amazing wife, Chelsa, without whom this book might never have even gotten off the ground.

Thanks to MATITU for making sure our business kept rocking while I was working on the book, and for all the help making sure its message gets heard.

Finally, I want to thank all the "Love Bunnies" that have attended my live events over the years, or hired me personally. Without you, this material never would have come through me to share with you and now with the world.

ABOUT THE AUTHOR

Christian Mickelsen is a leading authority on personal development and personal coaching, and the CEO of Future Force, Inc. He is the best-selling author of *How to Quickly Get Started as a Personal Coach*, *Get Clients Today*, and *Change the World*. As a personal coach for over 17 years and a trainer of coaches, he is on a mission to heal the world, and has helped countless thousands experience the life-changing power of coaching. He currently lives in San Diego, California, with his wife and three daughters.

If you'd like to get healing for yourself, become a healer, or turn your healing gifts into a successful business that helps heal the world, visit www.ChristianMickelsen.com to get involved.

NOTES

NOTES

Hay House Titles of Related Interest

YOU CAN HEAL YOUR LIFE, the movie,
starring Louise Hay & Friends
(available as a I-DVD program, an expanded
2-DVD set, and an online streaming video)
Learn more at www.hayhouse.com/louise-movie

THE SHIFT, the movie, starring Dr. Wayne W. Dyer
(available as a I-DVD program, an expanded
2-DVD set, and an online streaming video)
Learn more at www.hayhouse.com/the-shift-movie

❦

*THE LAW OF ATTRACTION: The Basics of the Teachings
of Abraham,* by Esther and Jerry Hicks

*E-SQUARED: Nine Do-It-Yourself Energy Experiments that
Prove Your Thoughts Create Your Reality,* by Pam Grout

All of the above are available at your local bookstore,
or may be ordered by contacting Hay House (see next page).

❦

We hope you enjoyed this Hay House book. If you'd like to receive our online catalog featuring additional information on Hay House books and products, or if you'd like to find out more about the Hay Foundation, please contact:

Hay House, Inc., P.O. Box 5100, Carlsbad, CA 92018-5100
(760) 431-7695 or (800) 654-5126
(760) 431-6948 (fax) or (800) 650-5115 (fax)
www.hayhouse.com® • www.hayfoundation.org

๛

Published in Australia by: Hay House Australia Pty. Ltd.,
18/36 Ralph St., Alexandria NSW 2015
Phone: 612-9669-4299 • *Fax:* 612-9669-4144
www.hayhouse.com.au

Published in the United Kingdom by: Hay House UK, Ltd.,
The Sixth Floor, Watson House, 54 Baker Street, London W1U 7BU
Phone: +44 (0)20 3927 7290 • *Fax:* +44 (0)20 3927 7291
www.hayhouse.co.uk

Published in India by: Hay House Publishers India,
Muskaan Complex, Plot No. 3, B-2, Vasant Kunj, New Delhi 110 070
Phone: 91-11-4176-1620 • *Fax:* 91-11-4176-1630
www.hayhouse.co.in

๛

Access New Knowledge.
Anytime. Anywhere.

Learn and evolve at your own pace
with the world's leading experts.

www.hayhouseU.com

Hay House Podcasts
Bring Fresh, Free Inspiration Each Week!

Hay House proudly offers a selection of life-changing audio content via our most popular podcasts!

Hay House Meditations Podcast

Features your favorite Hay House authors guiding you through meditations designed to help you relax and rejuvenate. Take their words into your soul and cruise through the week!

Dr. Wayne W. Dyer Podcast

Discover the timeless wisdom of Dr. Wayne W. Dyer, world-renowned spiritual teacher and affectionately known as "the father of motivation." Each week brings some of the best selections from the 10-year span of Dr. Dyer's talk show on Hay House Radio.

Hay House Podcast

Enjoy a selection of insightful and inspiring lectures from Hay House Live events, listen to some of the best moments from previous Hay House Radio episodes, and tune in for exclusive interviews and behind-the-scenes audio segments featuring leading experts in the fields of alternative health, self-development, intuitive medicine, success, and more! Get motivated to live your best life possible by subscribing to the free Hay House Podcast.

Find Hay House podcasts on iTunes, or visit
www.HayHouse.com/podcasts for more info.

Printed in the United States
by Baker & Taylor Publisher Services